The Flying S
By
Francis X King

From the editor of the *Grimoire of Armadel* and the author of *Sexuality, Magic and Perversion*. This is the story of the enigmatic eighteenth-century sorcerer whose work still influences occultists today. Francis Barrett was the first magician since the middle ages to compile a manual or 'grimoire' of magick. His *Magus or Celestial Intelligencer* is probably only surpassed by Aleister Crowley's *Magick in Theory and Practice*.

Francis King offers a fascinating picture of Francis Barrett, a man who lived on the frontier of technology, both in terms of the inner landscape and his pioneering experiments in balloon flight. He discusses Barrett's teachers, peers and the subsequent progress of his disciples. *The Flying Sorcerer* includes a previously unpublished Barrett manuscript on Crystal Vision, which was essential reading for the students of Barrett's magical school.

The Flying Sorcerer
Being
The magical and aeronautical adventures
of Francis Barrett, author of *The Magus*

By
Francis X King

Mandrake

First Edition 1992
(c) Mandrake 1992 and Francis X King

All rights reserved. No part of this publication may be reproduced or transmitted in any form or by any means, electronic or mechanical, including photocopy, recording, or an other information storage and retrieval system, without permission in writing from the publisher.

Other books written or edited by the same author include:
Astral Projection, Magic and Alchemy—Golden Dawn Instructional Manuscripts
Encyclopedia of Mind Mysteries and Magic
Grimoire of Armadel
Hermes and Eros—A Study in Sexuality, Magic and Perversion
Magic—The Western Tradition
Modern Ritual Magic
Rebirth of Magic (with Isabel Sutherland)
Rites of Modern Occult Magic
Rudolf Steiner and Holistic Medicine
Tantra for Westerners
Techniques of High Magic (with Stephen Skinner)

This monograph is dedicated to the memories of F. Israel Regardie and Gerald Yorke

The author thanks Timothy d'Arch Smith and Ron Heisler for information and stimulating conversation on the subjects of Francis Barrett and his writings, Chris Morgan of Mandrake for his patience, and the staff of the Library of the Wellcome Institute for their helpfulness.

King, Frances X
Francis Barrett.
1. Occultism
I. Title
133.092
ISBN 1-86992-820-2

Preface

During World War II somebody employed at Penguin Books decided that their list ought to include a title devoted to what was then generally referred to by that now unfashionable term 'the occult'. Accordingly an approach was made to that seemingly credulous Catholic paedophile, Montague Summers, a man whose studies of Restoration drama were little read and was then best known—as today he is best remembered—as the author of such books as *The Geography of Witchcraft* and *The Vampire*.

Summers was not the man to turn down any literary commission and, accordingly, he contracted to write a book to be entitled *Witchcraft and Black Magic*. He delivered his manuscript late, which probably irritated the editorial staff at Penguin, and it was not at all to the liking of those who read it.

Quite what Penguin had expected to receive is unclear—perhaps something on the same wavelength as the writings of the late Margaret Murray and her disciples or, more probably, a popularly written but scholarly refutation of Dr Murray's delightful but unsubstantiated theories.

What they in fact got was a sensationally written rehash of parts of Summers' earlier books which was characterized by both a total acceptance of the truth of all witchcraft confessions and a proclaimed belief in the literal correctness of the unpleasant teachings of Renaissance theologians in relation to both witchcraft and black magic.

Penguin were not amused and Montague Summers' manuscript was returned to its author[1], who found a more tolerant—or more enterprising—publisher in the Editor of *The Occult Review*, Ralph Shirley of Rider & Company.

In 1946 the book appeared under the Rider imprint. I acquired a copy soon after its publication and, whatever its faults, loved it—warts and all. I was intrigued by Summers' account of Francis Barrett's *The Magus* (1801) and was particularly impressed by his assertion of the existence of a tradition that the portraits of demons which were included in its illustrations were 'drawn from life'. Summers reproduced one of these depictions of those whom he somewhere else referred to as 'the aristocracy of hell' in *Witchcraft and Black Magic* and I was struck by the benignity of the being's appearance. He (or perhaps It) looked quite as pleasant as most of the schoolmasters with whom I was, or had been, acquainted and *much* nicer than any one of my male relations.

I was also awed by another illustration from *The Magus* which Summers thought worthy of reproduction; this was the delineation of the paraphernalia to be used by the magician for '*Invocation by the Chrystal* (sic)'. My imagination was sufficiently stirred by it to induce me to draw the other side of Barrett's portrayal of *'The Magic Wand to be used in Invocation...'*, complete with the inscription prescribed by Barrett (*Ego Alpha et Omega*), on a blank page of my Latin exercise book. My teacher noted this unorthodox addition to the lined pages intended to be devoted to such matters as the wall-building proclivities of Balbus but, being a man of unusual tolerance, merely wrote beside my drawing the stern injunction 'Vade Retro Satanas'.

I was consciously amused by this but may have been a little frightened on an unconscious level, for I immediately lost interest in both Barrett and *The Magus* for a period of ten years or so. When my interest in the man and his work reignited towards the end of the 1950s I tried to find out something more about Barrett than Summers' book had told me but was almost completely unsuccessful. All I could learn amounted to vague traditions that Francis Barrett had been an occult pupil of Ebenezer Sibley. At the time I uncritically accepted the truth of these legends. Subsequently I came to reject them although, as readers of this book will discover for themselves, I now think that the circumstantial evidence is such that in all probability the 'legend' is based on historical fact. Traditions on their own, however, amounted to very little and to me the author of *The Magus* appeared to be a man of mystery who had come from nowhere, written and published an extraordinary book, and vanished into a metaphorical or actual darkness. I concerned myself with other things.

Thirty years or so later I read both Timothy d'Arch Smith's essay on *The Magus*, included in the first edition of his *Books of the Beast*, and an illuminating article on Barrett written by the occult historian Ron Heisler. These sufficed to revive my juvenile Barrettophilia and I made some efforts to come to an understanding of both the psychology of the self-proclaimed Rosicrucian who compiled *The Magus* and the nature of his sources. This short book, *The Flying Sorcerer*, is the fruit of those efforts.

FXK

(1) As Timothy d'Arch Smith, Summers' bibliographer, has pointed out to me, there is good evidence that the planned Penguin edition of *Witchcraft and Black Magic* had reached page proofs by the summer of 1943; thus it seems likely that the Company's fairly costly decision to abandon its planned publication was taken at a very high level.

Contents

	Preface	v
1.	The Flying Sorcerer	9
2.	The Sorcerer's Apprentice	39

Illustrations
Francis Barrett's Portrait   viii
Page from Barrett's manuscript   37
J. P. Kellerman's Horoscope   38

Appendices
A. Barrett's Hitherto Unpublished
   Skrying Manuscript   53

B. J. P. Kellerman and
   Late Georgian Alchemy   67

Index   75

The engraving of Francis Barrett 'Student in Chemistry... & Occult Philosophy' which appeared as the frontispiece of the original 1801 edition of The Magus. *The fashion of Barrett's dress is in accordance with the date of the book's publication, so it is apparent that he compiled it when still a comparatively young man.*

Chapter One
The Flying Sorcerer

...a man whose reputation rightly lies solely with *The Magus*... a man of one book, a book which mirrors the extraordinarily important and far-reaching Gothic revival at the time of its publication, but heralds the revival of occultism in England and remains a source book of the highest importance to students of the present day.

So Timothy d'Arch Smith concluded his essay on Francis Barrett, compiler of *The Magus*, a book which was originally published in 1801 but is still used as a Do-It-Yourself guide to ceremonial magic by some occultists of the present day.[1]

Robert Southey (1774-1843), whose letters were often as amusing as his poetry was boring, took a very different view of Barrett and his book from that of Mr d'Arch Smith. Writing to his wife on 23 September 1802 he described how:

...We dined in the travellers' room at Swansea. There came in after dinner the balloon adventurer Barrett to sponge a glass of wine. Tell King I have seen a greater rogue than Solomon. This same Barrett who took in the people at Greenwich—and who wrote a book called the *Magus*—of

Chapter One

which I have seen the title page and his own rascally portrait as frontispiece. My gentleman professes to teach the occult sciences. Unhappily I did not know this was the fellow when I saw him—else I would have gone thro his sciences—and he puts all the letters in the alphabet after his name to look like honorary titles. A dog—he had better break his neck from a balloon to save the country the expense of hanging him.[2]

Southey's choleric letter shows that his memory of the title page of *The Magus* was defective. Barrett did not put 'all the letters in the alphabet after his name'—merely the initials 'F.R.C'. Southey was equally at fault in his implication that Barrett used these initials in the hope that the unwary might be deluded into thinking that he was an F.R.S., a Fellow of the Royal Society. The meaning of F.R.C. would have been apparent to many, perhaps most, of those who bought *The Magus*. These initials unquestionably stood for *Frater Roseae Crucis*, 'Brother of the Rosy Cross', and by employing them Francis Barrett was clearly making some sort of claim to a Rosicrucian initiation, to being possessed of the supposed secrets of the legendary fraternity which had intrigued European occultists for almost three centuries and still intrigues many of them at the present day.[3]

Southey was justified in calling Barrett 'the balloon adventurer', but only in the most literal sense—that the compiler of *The Magus* was a man who wished to adventure in balloons. The suggestion of some act of roguery by which Barrett had 'took in the people at Greenwich' was quite unfounded.

Nevertheless, Barrett had been the protagonist in a ballooning fiasco at Greenwich which had extended over two days and resulted in a number of people getting either their pockets picked or their heads broken.

The affair had begun in July 1802 with Barrett announcing his intention of making an aeronautical ascent from Greenwich (now part of London but at the time still separated from the metropolis by open countryside) on August 11 in a large hydrogen filled balloon of his own manufacture.

Barrett's announcement attracted a remarkable response. According to *The Times* of August 13 1802:

The roads leading from London... were filled the whole of

The Flying Sorcerer

the afternoon with conveyances of every description... Blackheath resembled a race-ground, carriages were continuously passing over it....

The crowd, so large that soldiers had been called in to control it, was to be disappointed—Barrett was finding it impossible to inflate his balloon by the method he was using in order to generate hydrogen from the chemical reaction of 'oil of vitriol', that is, sulphuric acid, with iron filings.

In theory the technique was simple enough. Huge casks, of the type manufactured for the storage of beer, were filled with a mixture of oil of vitriol and water—it was unsafe to use the vitriol in its concentrated form as it so speedily attacked the joints between the wooden staves of the casks that serious leaks were likely to develop. To the mixture were added iron filings and the casks were then sealed save for a small hole at the top into which tubes—Francis Barrett's were made of tin—were introduced.

The vitriol then reacted with the iron filings to produce hydrogen and a solution of ferrous sulphate in water, the former being, so it was hoped, conducted to the balloon through the tubes and inflating it.

The problems with this technique were two in number. Firstly, a certain amount of vaporized sulphuric acid tended to be carried over with the hydrogen and to attack both the soldered joints of the tin tubes and the fabric of the balloon itself, thus reducing its efficiency as a gas container. This, in any case, was not particularly high—all balloons of the period leaked hydrogen to some extent.

In his attempt to inflate his balloon Barrett was trying to generate hydrogen at sufficient speed to exceed the loss of the gas through the tubes and the balloon fabric. He failed and, probably fearing a riot, announced that the ascent would unfailingly be made at 3pm on the following day.

The gathering, which seems to have either been of a more amiable disposition than most Georgian crowds or overawed by the presence of the gunners who had been drafted in from the Royal Artillery depot at Woolwich in order to deal with any commotions, took its disappointment in good part and dispersed.

Barrett and his assistants worked until nine in the evening, presumably endeavouring to both improve the hydrogen-generating

11

Chapter One

equipment and to reduce the porosity of the balloon by coating its fabric with more of the 'elasticated substance' with which it was painted. They seem to have met with little success and at the instigation of the Chevalier Andrade, who had made available the grounds of his house for the planned ascent, the assistance of a certain Captain Sowden—supposedly an expert on balloon inflation—was called upon.

Captain Sowden confidently announced that if his directions were followed all would be well. Throughout the night he superintended labourers in the overhaul of the hydrogen generating and collecting apparatus and he also arranged for the balloon to be inflated with ordinary air pumped into it by two blacksmiths' bellows. This was presumably done in order to enable the detection and repair of particularly leaky areas of the fabric.

On the following day an enormous crowd gathered. According to *The Times* some of those present were expecting to witness a balloon ascent, others were unsure as to what would happen, and a third group were quite confident that there would be no ascent but were hoping for a riot. The latter seem to have included a notorious gang of pickpockets from London which, not long before, had made rich pickings from the crowd which had gathered to watch a balloon ascent made by M. Garnerin from the neighbourhood of the cricket pitch at Lords. It is to be presumed that the gang members were hoping for an equally profitable outing to Greenwich.

At around 2pm, reported *The Times*:

>...the tops of every house in sight of MR. ANDRADE'S ground were crowded with people, as well as several scaffolds erected in the gardens and adjacent premises. A large shed, belonging to a blacksmith, on which a number of persons had been permitted to stand, fell shortly after this period, with a tremendous crash, which alarmed every one who witnessed the accident, as it was known that there were also many persons under it at the time, and nothing less was thought but that many persons must have been killed, or had their limbs broken, when it miraculously turned out that the whole injury sustained was a few slight bruises.

At 3pm—the hour at which Barrett had promised to make his ascent—the balloon was moved on to a large wooden platform, connected

The Flying Sorcerer

to the casks in which the hydrogen was being generated, and the attempt at inflation begun.

The inflation procedure moved forward with painful slowness, presumably as a consequence of leaks from both Barrett's generating apparatus and the fabric of his balloon, and by five o'clock, at which time fresh oil of vitriol was added to the casks, it had become obvious to most that if any balloon ascent was to be made at all that day it would not be until the evening.

By seven o'clock the more lumpen proletarian elements of the crowd had grown unruly and, in spite of the attempts to keep the peace made by the artillerymen from Woolwich, a mob estimated at some five thousand in number had invaded the Chevalier Andrade's grounds and found amusement in stealing his fruit and uprooting the shrubs and saplings in his garden.

The London pickpockets took full advantage of the disorder. Thus, for example, Mr Madox, a brewer from London's Tooley Street—it was almost certainly he who had supplied the casks in which Barrett was generating his hydrogen—had what was the then considerable sum of five guineas neatly removed from his pocket as he stood on the platform by the balloon.

There seemed to be a strong possibility of riot and loss of life and it was determined that some sort of an ascent should be attempted even though the balloon was hardly half inflated.

Captain Sowden, Francis Barrett and Mr Madox got into the basket of the balloon and cast off the ropes which were supposedly holding it down. Nothing happened.

Captain Sowden and Mr Madox decided that Francis Barrett should make his flight alone and got out of the basket. Again nothing happened and Barrett remained obstinately earthbound. It was decided to send up the balloon without any passengers at all; so limited was its lifting power that even its wicker basket was too heavy for its capacities. Consequently the basket was removed and replaced with a child's cradle to which was attached a stream of flags.

At last the balloon rose from its platform and, watched by the mob who, for the moment, ceased their violent depredations, made a rapid ascent. After about ten minutes, said *The Times*, the balloon ceased to be visible and:

13

Chapter One

...speculative opinions were made as to what country it would pass into, and what the idea of the people would be who first found it, on seeing the child's cradle.

In fact Barrett's unladen balloon only remained aloft for half an hour or so, travelling about three miles in that time, and on the following day was retrieved by its owner from the marshland in which its flight had ended.

Barrett's failure made him the butt of much ridicule, probably typified by an unkind comment in *The Times* of August 18 1802:

> The art of puffing is now carried to such perfection that it is a shame for an Apothecary to appear ignorant in any species of it. Several of our Quacks have blown themselves higher than this occult Philosopher was able to send up his empty cradle.

By the time this paragraph was printed Barrett, his wife Grace, and his one year old son—another Francis—had already left London for Devon. From there they took passage in a small coasting vessel, arriving in Swansea on the last day of August.

He and his family took up residence with a local linen draper named Griffith and waited for the arrival of the balloon and the equipment used for hydrogen generation—for some reason these were being sent to Swansea by road under the care of a person to whom Barrett rather grandly referred as 'a trusted servant'.

Barrett whiled away his time by manufacturing 'Montgolfiers', in other words, hot air balloons. The first of these was made of tissue paper and, being some eighteen feet in diameter, was sufficiently large for Barrett to believe that it would be capable of lifting two animals, a cat and a dog, in its basket. A platform was erected in the Ball Court of the George Inn and a large crowd gathered to watch the planned ascent, which was intended to culminate with the cat and dog descending to earth by means of an automatic parachute of Barrett's own devising.

It was probably fortunate for the animals that, a short time before they were due to be launched into the air, Barrett found a large hole about half way up the balloon. This meant that only the upper half of it could be filled with hot air and that it had insufficient lifting power to carry even small animals.

It was decided that the balloon should be sent up as it was; for a

The Flying Sorcerer

minute or so it rose slowly through the air, then was caught by the wind, turned on its side and burst into flames.

Barrett, who seems to have been of remarkably resilient character, manufactured two smaller hot air balloons which made successful ascents within an hour of one another. Mercifully enough no passengers, canine or feline, were carried.

A day or two later Barrett's balloon and his hydrogen generating apparatus arrived, the tin tubes of the latter having been damaged on the journey and needing extensive repair.

By this time the would-be aeronaut was running out of money. He decided to hire the Ball Court of the George Inn and charge an admittance fee to those who wished to see him blowing up his balloon with a pair of blacksmiths' bellows. Not a very exciting exhibition, one imagines, and certainly an unprofitable one. In Barrett's own words:

> ...I began to have it inflated in the morning, and after half a day's puffing and blowing with a small pair of forge bellows, which had twenty holes in them, we got it about seven-tenths full; the day's exhibition yielded twenty-two shillings... A day or two after I began to fill it again with common air... the amount of this day's receipts was four shillings, out of which I had to pay, for workmen's labour, use of the Court etc. etc. about four pounds, twelve shillings and two-pence halfpenny, and I had about eleven shillings left to pay it with.

Barrett's predicament was such that, according to his own account, he considered setting himself up as a manufacturer of waterproof bathing caps and umbrellas, using the fabric of his balloon as raw material.

Instead he raised a subscription, had his tin tubes repaired, purchased quantities of oil of vitriol from Bristol and Neath, and announced that he would make a balloon ascent on October 6. The Swansea correspondent of *The Times* reported the events of that day as follows:

> The Balloon was to ascend at a quarter past one o'clock... The day was fine as could be wished... They began to fill the Balloon about eight o'clock; from that to eleven they got on but very slowly. At this time a complete stop was put to the process by the want of vitriol. The Chemist, who had let Mr

Chapter One

Barrett have 600 weight, would not furnish any more without the cash. Time was now getting on; the Balloon had no appearance of any thing being in it; messages and messengers now passed between Mr Barrett and the chemist until three o'clock, when the assemblage of persons on the spot (at least eight thousand) began to be unruly. Mr Barrett now came forward on the stage to make an apology, when just as he said—'Ladies and Gentlemen'—down fell the stage with a most tremendous crash, and Mr Barrett and his Balloon with it, with a great number of persons. Many were severely hurt. One boy had his legs broke; the Balloon was torn in its fall, and Mr Barrett was hurt. He now attempted to harangue the populace... hootings and howlings were the result.

Barrett was annoyed by this report, which he described as 'very incorrectly stated... not to say malicious or ill-natured'. The boy, he said, had only broken one of his legs and in any case he himself would meet the expense of having the limb set.

However loud the hoots and howlings of the mob may have been there were still some persons of substance who had confidence in Barrett and his balloon. A fresh subscription was raised. Enormous quantities of vitriol were purchased and Barrett applied to the balloon a coating of a faintly mysterious 'elastic gum varnish' of his own manufacture. At 8am on Friday October 16 the balloon began to be inflated—or so said the correspondent of *The Times*. According to Barrett, however, the process was commenced an hour and three-quarters later. Whatever the truth of the matter there seems to be no doubt that the inflation went well enough until the early afternoon, when a barrel of vitriol burst and, almost simultaneously, the wind tore a hole in the balloon's fabric, occasioning a considerable loss of gas.

Hasty repairs were made and fresh hydrogen generated. By three o'clock all supplies of vitriol were exhausted and, although the balloon was only partially inflated, Barrett entered its basket, and, after taking on board fifty pounds of ballast, a bottle of brandy, a loaf of bread and a pound of cold roast mutton, cast off the mooring ropes.

Nothing happened.

Barrett threw out his ballast, his bread and his mutton—wisely, he retained the brandy—and the balloon rose into the air and moved off, borne by the breeze, in the direction of a row of tall trees. It failed to clear them and came to the ground. The onlookers carried both Barrett and the balloon as far as possible from the trees and Barrett recommenced his flight.

The balloon ascended majestically into the air; Barrett waved his cap to the multitude below; the balloon immediately began to descend, coming to earth four fields or so away from its starting point. What followed is best told in Barrett's own words. The balloon:

...alternately ascended and descended for the space of a quarter of an hour, carrying me over fields, trees and hedges, and sometimes skimming a few feet above the surface of the earth.

From this it is clear that Barrett almost succeeded in making a proper ascent—the lifting power of the balloon almost exactly matched the weight of Barrett and the basket in which he stood. If he had been a few pounds lighter—fully dressed he weighed 130 pounds—or if he had been able to continue the process of inflation for another half hour or so, he would almost certainly have achieved his aim, 'to be abandoned to a new element'.

As soon as Barrett tired of his hedge hopping and left the basket of the balloon the latter made a rapid ascent. It stayed aloft for three hours and came to earth some six miles or so away where it was found by two labourers who imagining, so they said, that Barrett was trapped inside the balloon, cut it in half with the object of releasing him.

All Francis Barrett's ballooning endeavours, however farcically they may have ended, were marked by a boldness bordering on recklessness—by a readiness to undertake tasks beyond his capabilities. The same character trait was also apparent in both the way he compiled *The Magus*, his textbook of alchemy, divination and ceremonial magic, and in his attempt to set himself up as a teacher of all the occult arts, from scrying to the ritual evocation of spiritual beings to visible appearance, in Marylebone.

In his essay on Francis Barrett and *The Magus* Timothy d'Arch Smith observed that by 1800 Gothic romanticism had arrived at a stage where:

Magic was in the air, a return to the practices and philosophies

Chapter One

of the medieval adepts was demanded, it was time for the true Rosicrucian, in the person of Francis Barrett, to come into the open and show the way.

Barrett's *Magus* is unique in being the only attempt—at a time when interest was ripe—to revive the mysteries of magic, and he clearly spent long hours toiling over translations of qabalistic and occult lore which had never before been translated into English or were issued in the seventeenth century and were then, as now, of the last rarity.

It is apparent from *The Magus* that it was the seventeenth century translations mentioned by Mr d'Arch Smith to which Barrett gave most of his attention.

Thus, for example, Book II, Part II of *The Magus*, which Barrett entitled 'The Perfection And Key Of The Cabala Or Ceremonial Magic' and presented as though it were a composition of his own, was no more than a slightly modified and modernized version of the English translation of Cornelius Agrippa's *Fourth Book Of Occult Philosophy* which had been made by Robert Turner and published by a London bookseller in 1655.

Barrett took slightly more trouble with Book II Part III of *The Magus* which is a translation of the *Heptameron* (also known as *The Magical Elements*) attributed to Peter de Abano (*c.1250-c.1317*). Here Barrett also used a seventeenth century translation, again by Robert Turner, but he did at least translate most of the conjurations in it from the Latin in which Turner had thought fit to leave them.

Almost all of *The Magus* does, in fact, seem to have been derived from earlier printed and manuscript English translations of medieval and renaissance texts. I strongly suspect, for example, that pages 165-8 of Book I of *The Magus* are no more than a Barrettian recension of an earlier English abridgement, in English translation, of Peter de Abano's *Liber Experimentorum*... a book which described 'wonderful experiments with rings according to the 28 mansions of the moon' and was concerned with an astrological variety of talismanic magic originally derived from Arab sources. Similarly, Part I of Book II of *The Magus* seems to consist largely of a paraphrase of parts of John Heydon's *Harmony Of The World* (1662)—or, as Heydon himself was in the habit of publishing other men's works under his own name (as he did with

The Flying Sorcerer

Francis Bacon's *New Atlantis*), perhaps both writers were drawing on the same source.

Barrett's real offence was neither his use of the work of earlier translators nor his modernizations of their already somewhat archaic English. It was that he had recklessly produced a work which incorporated in almost their entirety some of the great classics of European occult literature *without any indication at all that he had not written them himself.*

It seems a virtual certainty that Barrett personally owned neither printed nor manuscript versions of most of the treatises from which *The Magus* was compiled. According to a note copied from a manuscript of Frederick Hockley (1808-1885) by the collector of occult manuscripts whom Mr d'Arch Smith refers to in his *Books Of The Beast* as 'Frater N' all of Barrett's source material was lent to him by the occult bookseller John Denley (1764-1842). Hockley wrote that all that is of real value in *The Magus* is:

> ...taken from C. Agrippa and the Clavis or Key to unlock the Mysteries of Rabbi Solomon, and an ancient work on Telesmata of great rarity which only exists in MS of which, however, there are a large number of copies extant. For compiling this book my late friend John Denley, the Occult Bookseller of Catherine Street, lent Barrett the whole of the materials.[4]

There are certain puzzling features about Hockley's note. It is hard to understand, for example, how he could describe a work as being 'of great rarity' and then, in the same sentence, state that there 'are a large number of copies extant'. His statement that all that is of real value in the book is taken from Agrippa and the *Clavis* seems almost equally odd; I can only assume that, for some reason of his own, Hockley had decided that the magic of the *Heptameron* was worthless.

With all such provisos there is no reason to doubt that, while Hockley could have had no first hand knowledge of the circumstances in which *The Magus* was compiled (it was, after all, published seven years or so before he was born), Denley had told him that it was he who had supplied Francis Barrett with his raw materials and that Denley was telling the truth.

This is a strong indication that at the time of the compilation of *The*

19

Chapter One

Magus John Denley was on remarkably good terms with Francis Barrett—for, in later life at least, Denley seems to have been unwilling to even sell the rarer items in his stock, let alone lend them to others. Bulwer Lytton described this characteristic of Denley in the following passage from the introduction to his occult novel *Zanoni*:

...an old bookshop, existing some years since in the neighbourhood of Covent Garden... there was little enough to attract the many in those precious volumes which the labour of a life had accumulated on the shelves of my old friend D[enley]... the curious might discover the most notable collection ever amassed by an enthusiast of the works of the Alchemist, Cabalist, and Astrologer. The owner had lavished a fortune on the purchase of unsaleable treasures. But old D[enley] did not desire to sell. It absolutely went to his heart when a customer entered his shop; he watched the movements of the presumptuous intruder with a vindictive glare, he fluttered around him with uneasy vigilance; he frowned, he groaned, when profane hands dislodged his idols from their niches. If it were one of the favourite sultanas of his wizard harem that attracted you and the price named were not sufficiently enormous, he would not unfrequently double the sum. Demur, and in brisk delight he snatched the venerable charmer from your hands; accede, and he became the picture of despair... A believer himself in his Averroes and Paracelsus, he was as loth as the philosophers he studied to communicate to the profane the learning he had collected.

While Bulwer Lytton no doubt exaggerated the unwillingness of Denley to sell his stock his description was based on reality; either Denley's nature had completely changed over the quarter of a century or so between the compilation of *The Magus* and Lytton making his acquaintance or, as I have suggested, in 1800 Denley and Barrett enjoyed a close relationship with one another. If this was the case they soon fell out if Hockley's note is to be believed, for he recorded that Denley complained that Barrett 'never recompensed him with even a copy' of *The Magus*.

While *The Magus* was a compilation, and while Barrett rarely

The Flying Sorcerer

made it at all clear to his readers that he was doing no more than paraphrasing earlier English translations of occult texts, it would be unreasonable to regard him as no more than an impudent plagiarist with a flare for publicity.

He was a synthesizer of talent, even genius, and in *The Magus* he combined and harmonized a large number of texts, varying in date from the fourteenth to the early eighteenth century, in such a way that they provided a very adequate Do-It-Yourself textbook of ritual and talismanic magic.

From one of the notes to *The Magus* it is also clear that Barrett was a man who, while wanting to be a 'natural philosopher'—as was evinced by his ballooning adventures—was prepared to accept the truth of ancient folk beliefs provided they were vaguely explicable in terms of 'vital spirits' or 'magnetism'.

The note in question is to be found on page sixteen of Book II, Part I and is a comment on a passage—taken, so I believe, from a seventeenth century English translation of one of the Paracelsian treatises of J. B. van Helmont (1577-1644)—dealing with the alleged occult properties of human blood.

The passage on which Barrett commented read as follows: 'For there are in the blood certain vital powers, the which, as if they were soulified or enlivened, do demand revenge from Heaven, yea, and judicial punishment from earthly judges on the murderer...'.

In Barrett's note on van Helmont's assertion he recorded a personal experience:

> This singular property of the blood, which Helmont calls Vital Powers, is no less wonderful than true, having been myself a witness of this experiment while in South Wales. It was tried upon a body that had been maliciously murdered, through occasion of a quarrel over-night at an alehouse. The fellow who was suspected of the murder appeared the next day in public seemingly unconcerned. The Coroner's Jury sat upon the body within twenty-four hours after this notable murder was committed; when the suspect was suddenly taken into custody and taken away to the same public-house where the inquisition was taken. After some debate, one Dr Jones desired the suspected to be brought into the room;

Chapter One

which done he desired the villain to lay his left hand under the wound, which was a deep gash on the neck, and another on the breast; the villain plainly confessed his guilt by his trepidation; but as soon as he lightly laid his finger on the body, the blood immediately ran, about six or seven drops, to the admiration of all present. If any one doubts the truth of this narrative... let him call personally upon me... and I will convince him of the fact.

Barrett's autobiographical note is of interest in several respects. Firstly it shows that he had visited South Wales at least two years or so before his ballooning exploits at Swansea; for reasons which will be made apparent later in this chapter I think it likely that, although he referred to himself as an Englishman, he was of Welsh extraction and that the 'Dr Jones' to whom he referred in his note *may* have been related to him. Secondly it shows that Barrett was a man attracted to curious occult experiments. Finally it reveals something about the folk culture of the time in which he lived and in which 'cunning men' and 'wise women' still flourished—that at around the end of the eighteenth century a Coroner could be persuaded to allow the ancient magical technique of what the Scots called 'bahr recht' (bier right) to be practised in his court.

This ancient test of guilt or innocence, by which suspects were compelled to touch the body of a supposed victim of murder in order to see if the corpse would bleed, had last been successfully employed in an English Coroner's court as long ago as 1623. On that occasion a Hertfordshire inquest had brought in a verdict of *felo de se*, 'self murder', in respect of a woman named Johane Norcott (or Norkott) who had been found dead in bed, with her throat cut and a bloody knife stuck into the floor of her room.

Almost a month afterwards the jury changed its mind[5] and ordered the exhumation of the body so that the dead woman's husband, mother-in-law, sister-in-law, and a relation of the husband by marriage should endure the ordeal of touching it.

The effects of their touching the corpse were dramatic:

...the brow of the dead which before was of a livid and carrion colour, begun to have a dew or gentle sweat arise upon it, which increased by degrees till the sweat ran down in drops on the face. The brow turned to a lively and fresh

The Flying Sorcerer

colour, and the deceased opened one of her eyes and shut it again; and this opening the eye was done three several times. She likewise thrust out the ring or marriage finger three times and pulled it in again, and the finger dropped blood from it on the grass.

All four were tried at Hertford Assizes—and acquitted by a sceptical jury. This verdict was largely overturned, however, at a new trial heard before the Lord Chief Justice in Lent 1629. This time the jury, no doubt impressed by the evidence of two parish priests who had witnessed the exhumation and stated ˇthat they had ascertained that the fluid which dropped from the corpse was, in truth, blood, found Arthur Norcott (the dead woman's husband), his mother and his sister guilty of murder. The first two were hanged; the second 'pleaded her belly', i.e. pregnancy, and was reprieved [6].

No doubt Francis Barrett witnessed many other occult experiments in circumstances rather less public than those in which he had seen a corpse bleed at its murderer's touch—but to what extent he had actually carried out the various rites and ceremonies of the magic with which he concerned himself is uncertain. It is sure, however, that he felt himself adequately qualified to give practical instruction in the occult arts and sciences, inserting the following advertisement at the end of Book II of *The Magus*:

> The Author of this Work respectfully informs those who are curious in the studies of Art and Nature, especially of Natural and Occult Philosophy, Chemistry, Astrology, etc. etc. that, having been indefatigable in his researches into these sublime Sciences, of which he has treated at large in this Book, that he gives private instructions and lectures upon any of the above-mentioned Sciences; in the course of which he will discover many curious and rare experiments. Those who become Students will be initiated into the choicest operations of Natural Philosophy, Natural Magic, the Cabala, Chemistry, the Talismanic Art, Hermetic Philosophy, Astrology, Physiognomy etc., etc. Likewise they will acquire the knowledge of the Rites, Mysteries, Ceremonies, and Principles of the ancient Philosophers, Magi, Cabalists, Adepts etc.,—The purpose of this School (which will consist of no greater

Chapter One

number than Twelve Students) being to investigate the hidden treasures of Nature; to bring the Mind to the contemplation of the Eternal Wisdom; to promote the discovery of whatever may conduce to the perfection of Man; the alleviating the miseries and calamities of this life, both in respect of ourselves and others; the study of religion and morality here, in order to secure ourselves felicity hereafter; and, finally, the promulgation of whatever may conduce to the general happiness and welfare of mankind—those who feel themselves thoroughly disposed to enter upon such a course of studies, as is above recited, with the same principles of philanthropy with which the Author invites the lovers of philosophy and wisdom, to incorporate themselves in so select, permanent, and desirable a society, may speak with the Author upon the subject, at any time between the hours of Eleven and Two o'clock, at 99 Norton Street, Mary-le-Bonne.

It is unlikely that Francis Barrett was fully qualified to teach all the occult techniques referred to in this puffing announcement—although he may well have been, as he himself claimed, acquainted with 'a vast number of curious experiments in occult and chymical operations, which have fell either under my own observation, or have been transmitted to me from others'. Certainly he seems to have himself performed the rituals involved in invoking spirits into a crystal, for in a didactic communication dated May 8 1802 ('in the day and hour of [Mercury]' i.e. either the first or eighth hour after sunrise on a Wednesday) he wrote that 'The Chrystal that is sent with few pages of <u>Mans.</u> was consecrated by me & made for my own particular use, & was shortly afterward borrowed by a Lady Aunt to a Disciple of mine....'.

Nevertheless, it is probably in the last phrase of the first quotation given in the preceding paragraph ('or have been transmitted to me by others') that its real significance lies in connection with the psychological state which induced Francis Barrett to set up his magical school.

In relationship to this reckless occult adventure it is worth considering the ballooning episodes which have already been described.

There is no doubt at all that Barrett had no practical experience of ballooning whatsoever, not even as a passenger on the briefest of flights,

The Flying Sorcerer

prior to the Greenwich fiasco described earlier; a written statement of his own makes this quite certain. It is very likely, however, that he had witnessed balloon ascents, several of which had been made in London not long prior to his own attempts, and that he had had 'transmitted to him by others' details of the technical processes involved in the manufacture and inflation of balloons filled with 'inflammable air'—hydrogen. Such transmitted knowledge, inadequate as it may well have been, was the only basis on which, with a confidence which was both splendid and foolish, Barrett embarked on a series of aeronautical adventures which made him the subject of general ridicule[7].

I think it almost certain that a similar over-confidence inspired Barrett to set himself up as a teacher in practical occultism. He was acquainted with the literature of the subject, knew men who had carried out the processes taught in that literature, and was, I suggest, so confident of his own theoretical knowledge of ceremonial techniques that he boldly offered to teach them to others.

This does not mean that he had never performed evocations or other occult experiments (such as the consecration of his crystal) and been present at such experiments when they had been carried out by others. It is safe to assume, however, that an occult tradition reported by the late Montague Summers, that the terrifying portraits of demons which illustrate *The Magus* had been drawn by Barrett 'from life' can be disregarded.

I do not think, however, that another tradition recorded by Summers in relation to Francis Barrett's magical school can be quite so easily discounted. Summers claimed that he had been told that some of Barrett's pupils:

> ...advanced far upon the path of transcendental wisdom. One at least was a Cambridge man, of what status—whether an undergraduate or the Fellow of a college—I do not know but there is reason to believe that he initiated others, and until quite recent years—it perhaps persists even today—the Barrett tradition was maintained at Cambridge, but very privately, and his teaching has been handed on to promising subjects.

In a most interesting article on Barrett published in the magazine *Pentacle* Mr Ron Heisler firmly rejected Summers' statement, asserting

Chapter One

that '...since the famed work actually announces the existence of Barrett's school at... Marylebone, Summers' initial comment was asinine to begin with'.

While it is quite possible that Summers invented his alleged 'Cambridge tradition' in order to chill his readers' blood—he was, after all, a Gothic enthusiast—I fail to see how the supposed tradition is intrinsically 'asinine' or even exceptionally improbable. While the Cambridge of 1801 was considerably less lax than the Oxford of the same period, there is no doubt that some Fellows—and perhaps some undergraduates—were able with impunity to absent themselves from their colleges for extended periods of time. If one such part-time absentee was a devotee of the occult tradition he might well have become one of Barrett's pupils. In any case at least one of Barrett's disciples was taught through the medium of instructional letters.

Whether or not there were one or more practitioners of ritual magic and other forbidden arts at work in early nineteenth century Cambridge[8] it seems certain that Francis Barrett found at least some pupils. Many years ago I was given a sight of papers and books which were apparently those of one such student. It is likely that these belonged to either an associate of 'Doctor' Parkins of Lincolnshire or to Parkins himself. For, as Mr Heisler has pointed out in his *Pentacle* article, a manuscript dating from 1802 which is held in the Library of the Wellcome Institute and is entitled *Directions For The Invocations of Spirits* contains a note which indicates that Parkins was a pupil of Barrett. In full this note reads:

> This most noble Science of Divine Magic, which is the highest Branches (sic) of Learning is regularly taught in all its parts by Dr. Parkins, Little Gonerly, near Grantham, Lincolnshire. Pupil to the late Mr. F. Barrett.

It is likely that the note was written by Parkins himself—particularly as on the last sheet of the MS there is a cursing spell and magical diagram of the type Parkins is known to have traded in.

Parkins was a most interesting occultist in that his activities exhibited what would seem to have been a blend of the traditional magic practised by the 'Cunning man' (or 'Wise woman') with an altogether more intellectual brand of esotericism. Before dealing with him, however, it is worth outlining such biographical details of the early life of Francis Barrett as are ascertainable.

The Flying Sorcerer

In his *Pentacle* article Mr Heisler included the following interesting passage:

> Barrett was already active in certain respects by 1780, for a manuscript by him of that date survives—a translation of *The rise and origin of common salt* by Georg von Welling.

In relation to this passage Mr Heisler has noted that MSS 127, 128 and 140 of the Mellon Collection 'show Barrett's handwriting in both 1780 and June 1801 in translations of the same von Welling work'.

If this was indeed so one would have to assume that the latest possible date for Francis Barrett's birth would have been about 1764 and that in all probability he was born several years earlier. There are, however, insuperable difficulties in accepting such an early date for Barrett's birth. The first is provided by the engraving of Barrett which is printed at the beginning of *The Magus*.

This, both drawn and engraved by Daniel Orme—an artist renowned for his accurate portrayals of reality—shows a man who is clearly no more than thirty years old, and perhaps considerably younger. The coat which Barrett is depicted as wearing in this engraving is, so I am assured by an expert in the history of costume, of a cut contemporary with the date of the publication of *The Magus*.

The second difficulty relates to Barrett's marriage, of which I provide details on a subsequent page. All I will say concerning this at this stage is that if Barrett was in truth the translator of the 1780 von Welling MS one would have to accept that in 1800 a mother gave her consent to the marriage of her sixteen year old daughter with a man at least twenty, and probably many more, years older than that daughter—possible but improbable unless the groom was a man of some wealth, which Barrett was not.

A third obstacle is created by the nature of Barrett's ballooning adventures. While these may have ended farcically they were extremely dangerous—quite a few early balloonists who employed hydrogen, as distinct from hot air, to give their vehicles the required 'lift' ended their lives in fire and explosion. Francis Barrett would have been aware of this and I think it intrinsically improbable that a man old enough to have been translating von Welling in 1780 would have risked his life in this way, particularly when he had a dependent wife and child.

What then of the supposed identity of the handwriting between

Chapter One

Mellon MSS 127, 128 and 140?

In fact L. C. Witten and R. Pachella, the editors of Volume IV of *Alchemy and the Occult* (Yale University Press), the catalogue of the Mellon Collection, did not claim that the handwriting used in the three MSS was identical. All that they asserted was that the MSS clearly belonged to the same family and that it would be 'tempting', in spite of the differences in orthography and handwriting between MSS 127-128 (which are both clearly from the same hand and have the same provenance) and MS 140, which is definitely in Barrett's hand, to think that the last is a revised version, by Barrett, of a translation he had made over twenty years earlier. In this connection they point out the identity of the curiously spelt phrase 'Kitchin salt' in both MS 128 and MS 140.

I am sure that the temptation referred to by Messrs Witten and Pachella must be resisted. Quite apart from the difficulties regarding Barrett's age which I have described above the title page of the 1802 Barrett MS (that is, Mellon MS 140) provides evidence that it is not a translation of Georg von Welling's treatise by Barrett, but merely a revision by him of an already existing translation.

On the title page in question, unquestionably written in Barrett's hand, the work is clearly described as a translation of von Welling *annotated and corrected* (my emphasis) by Francis Barrett. If the translation had been made by Barrett himself he would undoubtedly have said so—he was hardly the man to hide his light under a bushel.

I conclude that Mellon MS 140 is a reworking by Barrett of an earlier translation of von Welling, from which MS 128 also probably derives, of a sort essentially similar to the reworkings of Agrippa and Peter de Abano which I have described on an earlier page. Consequently I believe that the evidence provided by the portrait of Francis Barrett which appears at the front of *The Magus* is conclusive—in 1800 he was somewhere between twenty and thirty years of age.

The author of *The Magus*, then, would appear to be a man who was born between 1770 and 1780, and who probably had connections with both Marylebone, where he established his occult school, and Devon, from whence he, according to his own account, sailed to Swansea. According to the same account he also had a wife and child when he travelled to Swansea in 1802.

No doubt there were dozens of Francis Barretts born in the

eighteenth century—but the only one of whom I can find any record and who fits the required specification is a man born on December 18, 1774 and baptized at St Mary's Church, Marylebone in January 1775.

The parents of this Francis Barrett, whom I am reasonably certain was the author of *The Magus*, were recorded as Francis and Ann Barrett. I (somewhat tentatively) identify them with the Francis Barrett and Ann Jones who married at St Martin's in the Fields on September 29 1772— while the parishes of Marylebone and St Martin's in the Fields did not abut directly on one another they were very close indeed, and it is to be presumed that at some time between marriage and the birth of their son the Barretts moved a mile or two away. Barrett is a Welsh name and Jones, along with Evans and Thomas, is the commonest of Welsh names. However, if the couple who married at St Martin's in the Fields were, as I suspect, both Welsh and the parents of the author of *The Magus* it would explain the fact that the magician/balloonist visited Wales on at least two occasions—and it is not beyond conjecture that the Dr Jones whose experiment with the corpse of a murdered man was described in *The Magus* was in some way related to Barrett.

If my identification of the parents of the magician Francis Barrett is correct it is clear that his origins were comparatively humble. For at the time of his marriage to Ann Jones the elder Barrett was illiterate, signing his name with a cross. Interestingly enough Ann Jones was literate—not only did she sign the register (Anne (*sic*) Jones) but her signature displays a practised hand, i.e. that of someone used to writing, not that of someone whose sole claim to literacy was the ability to write a signature in large, clumsy pot-hooks of the sort quite often found in Parish Registers of the period.

Nothing is known—to me at any rate—of the life of Francis Barrett between his birth and his marriage on the 20 January 1800.

It seems likely, however, that he was apprenticed to an apothecary, for in 1802 he was described as 'an apothecary...' There seems to me some possibility that he also occupied some position connected with the shipping industry—it may be that he was a surgeon's mate or even a ship's surgeon—many who filled such offices lacked formal medical qualifications. Certainly details of the ballooning fiasco at Greenwich suggest that Barrett was accustomed to working with seamen and/or dockers. A connection with the sea may also be inferred from a very

29

Chapter One

curious note printed on page 119 of the first volume of *The Magus*. In this Barrett refers to a Doctor Edward Spry of Plymouth Dock (now Devonport) who had 'fell under my notice of late years'. Doctor Spry, whom Barrett referred to as 'Philosopher, Cabalist and Physician', was reputed to live upon 'a gooseberry a day in summer, and an oatcake and three glasses of white wine the rest of the season...'.

While I feel that Doctor Spry may have supplemented this odd diet with the occasional leg of mutton and even a loaf of bread—perhaps when other cabalists were not observing him—I see no good reason to doubt either his existence or that Francis Barrett was acquainted with him. It is difficult to account for this acquaintanceship save on the supposition that Barrett followed an occupation connected with the sea—the Plymouth Dock of the late eighteenth century was neither salubrious nor a place which any person of respectability would visit unless he had very good reason for so doing.

If Barrett *was* a surgeon's mate, or followed some other maritime occupation, it would account for the fact that his marriage took place in Barnstaple, which by the late eighteenth century was regaining some of its importance as a seaport, particularly as far as the coasting trade was concerned.[9]

One can be reasonably sure that Francis Barrett was not a long standing resident of Barnstaple at the time of his marriage because of the most unusual way in which that same marriage was recorded in the Parish Register.

Like a great many Marriage Registers of the time that of Barnstaple was in a semi-printed form. Each page was divided into a number of sections, one for each marriage. The first four lines of each section contained the printed words:

of th
and   of th
    were
married in this   by

The printed letters 'th' in lines 1 and 2 would have added to them either the letter 'e' or the letters 'is'. The first amendment was made when one of the parties to the marriage came from a Parish outside that in which that marriage was celebrated; the second when one or both of them came from the home Parish. As an example of how this worked

The Flying Sorcerer

I reproduce the first four lines of the entry in the Barnstaple Marriage Register for a marriage that took place a month or so after that of Barrett—italic letters indicate the part of the entry that was not printed but added in the handwriting of the Parish Clerk:

John Selly of the *parish of Emmore in the County of Somerset Bachelor* and *Elizabeth Gillard* of th*is parish Spinster* were married in this *Church* by *Banns*

Such a form as that illustrated above was standard not only in the Barnstaple Register but in all the semi-printed Registers of the period.

Francis Barrett, however, was recorded as being neither as '*of* this Parish' (my emphasis) nor 'of the Parish of so-and-so'. Instead the printed letters 'of th' in line I had been crossed out and the groom was described as 'Francis Barrett *resident in* (my emphasis) the parish of Barnstaple...'.

I am told by genealogists that this highly unusual amendment, by which Barrett is described as being resident *in* the Parish but not *of* the Parish, almost certainly indicates that he had only recently arrived in Barnstaple and had no intention of living there permanently. It was odd, however, that Barrett was not described as being 'of the Parish' in which he usually resided, for this statement of fact would normally have been recorded in the Register. The fact that it was not so recorded suggests that Barrett had no particular fixed abode at the time of his marriage—this may perhaps have indicated that, as I have already suggested, he pursued some sort of maritime occupation.

Barrett's wife, born Grace Hodge, was only sixteen years old at the time of her marriage and her signature in the Register was somewhat shaky and blotted—no doubt she had found the ceremony something of an ordeal. Barrett's own signature, however, was firm, clear and, most important of all, identical with two undoubtedly authentic signatures of the author of *The Magus* which are known to me.[10] The signatures of the two witnesses to the wedding were also clear. Unfortunately both were 'professional witnesses': men who were associated with the Church in some way (perhaps the Sexton and the Parish Clerk), one or both of whom signed as witness in a number of entries in the Register, and thus were clearly neither friends nor associates of Barrett.

It is unlikely that Francis Barrett and his young wife stayed long

Chapter One

in Barnstaple after their wedding. For their son, another Francis, born a respectable one year, one week and one day after the marriage, was baptized at St Mary's Church in Marylebone in January 1801.

While Francis Barrett was undoubtedly resident in Marylebone at the time of his son's baptism it is unlikely that he was yet living at 99 Norton Street, the address which was advertised in *The Magus* as that at which he was prepared to receive potential disciples.

A letter written by the astrologer 'Sepharial' (i.e. Walter Gorn Old, 1864-1929) in 1895 baldly asserted that at some time 'in the early 1800s' Barrett was living at Catherine Street, Cavendish Square. Whether he had knowledge of some evidence for this statement or whether he was merely repeating an occult tradition is of no great moment—for there is no good reason to doubt the essential truth of Sepharial's statement. For Catherine Street was not only in the parish in which Francis and Grace Barrett's son was baptized, but at the time Barrett was compiling Book I of *The Magus* he was undoubtedly living at Prince's Street (now John Prince's Street) which is within almost a stone's throw of Catherine Street. It may well be either that the Barretts resided, firstly, at Catherine Street and then moved a very short distance away to Prince's Street, or that Sepharial was recording a tradition which, while essentially correct, had become distorted in the course of time.

Whatever the truth of the matter may be what is beyond question is that the first (and unpublished) draft of the advertisement for occult pupils which Barrett inserted into *The Magus* and which I have reproduced in its last form on an earlier page establishes the magician/balloonist's residence in Prince's Street. This draft, worded much more modestly than the final version and not even making it clear that Barrett was offering occult tuition, read as follows:

Advertisement

> The Author having persons of respectability frequently calling upon him to converse upon the various Occult Subjects treated upon in this book most respectfully begs leave to request that they will condescend to communicate any subject of doubt and enquiry by letter post paid which will be attended to with the utmost punctuality, and every satisfaction given by letter in return; or otherwise he is most

at leisure from half past One O'Clock 'till 4 O'Clock in the afternoon, which Space of Time he will [be] able to devote to personal conversation upon scientific matters, with any person who may please to honour him with their attention.

Princes Street
Cavendish Square
London

This advertisement is crossed through in that part of Barrett's MS of *The Magus* which has survived and is today to be found in the Library of the Wellcome Institute. Clearly at some time between its drafting and the delivery of the MS to the printer Barrett and his family had migrated to 99 Norton Street where it seems likely that they rented a room, or rooms, rather than the whole house. For the tenant of the house was a certain Catherine Collier, on at least one occasion referred to as Catherin Coller, and it was she who paid the Parish Rates and the Land Tax.

It seems possible that Catherine Collier was either a pupil of Barrett or, perhaps, the 'aunt of a Disciple' to whom the magician had once lent his consecrated crystal. It is not beyond conjecture that she was the person referred to in a cryptic note—presumably an 'in joke'—on page 190 of Part II of *The Magus* concerning a lady who had purchased a portable anvil. Anvils, oddly, were used in some alchemical processes (as late as the 1930s a practising alchemist based at the Woking Mosque was using an anvil in the course of his mystic experiments in transmutation) and it seems unlikely that Francis Barrett's lady was intending to engage in the manufacture of horse-shoes.[11]

If Catherine Collier was neither a pupil of Francis Barrett nor a relation of one she was clearly a quite exceptionally tolerant landlady. For to allow a sub-tenant to not only establish an occult school in one's home but to openly advertise its existence would have been a most curious procedure in 1801—even at the present day it would be generally looked upon as a somewhat surprising one.

I know of no evidence whatsoever concerning Francis Barrett's activities after the ballooning exploits of 1802—unless, indeed, he was the author of *The Lives of Alchemical Philosophers* which was first printed by Lackington, Allen, under a variant title in 1814.

I am not qualified to form an opinion on whether Barrett was, or was not, the compiler of this muddled book.[12] Both Timothy d'Arch

Chapter One

Smith and the late A. E. Waite expressed the opinion that *The Magus* and *The Lives* were not compiled by the same man. Mr Ron Heisler, however, believes that they were. My personal attitude to the question of the authorship of *The Lives* is one of agnosticism. I cannot help wondering, however, whether even if Barrett was not the compiler of *The Lives* at least some manuscripts copied out by him from seventeenth century printed books were included in the section of *The Lives* which contains alchemical treatises; many of these come from sources with which it can be shown Francis Barrett was familiar.

NOTES

(1) Mr d'Arch Smith's essay on Francis Barrett, originally published in 1967, is most easily available in the first edition of his *Books of the Beast* (Aquarian Press, 1987). The essay has been omitted from the enlarged and revised second edition of the *Books of the Beast* (Mandrake 1992).

(2) The full text of the letter from which this quotation is taken will be found in *New Letters of Robert Southey 1792-1810* (Columbia University Press, 1965) Volume I. I am grateful to Mr Michael Cox, formerly of the Aquarian Press, for drawing my attention to this letter.

(3) In fact Barrett's use of the initials 'F.R.C.' on the title page of *The Magus* would appear to have been something of an afterthought, being added to the manuscript version of the title page at some time between its first drafting and its delivery to the printer. In this connection see Appendix A.

(4) At the period in which *The Magus* was being compiled Denley was not, of course, 'of Catherine Street'. At the time he seems to have been operating his bookselling activities from 10 Gate Street, Lincoln's Inn Fields.

(5) As the corpse was found with not only its throat cut but its neck broken it is extremely difficult to understand how the Coroner's Jury arrived at its original verdict.

(6) In the 1680s a trial for murder took place in Scotland at which almost the only evidence against the accused was the fact that the corpse of the victim bled at his touch. He was found guilty and executed. As in the English case of 1628 family feuds seem to have been involved; the victim was the father of the accused and the latter was strongly suspected of having an incestuous relationship with his own mother. Sir

The Flying Sorcerer

Walter Scott, who examined seventeenth century reports of the case, gave it as his opinion that these suspicions may well have been justified. It is perhaps worth adding that in February 1658 an attempt was made to prove Major George Strangeways, a member of a well known Dorset family, guilty of the murder of his brother in law, a Mr Fussel of Blandford, by compelling him to touch the two bullet wounds in the dead man's body. There was no bleeding—but on other evidence Strangeways was charged with murder. He refused to plead either Guilty or Not Guilty and, it being decided that he was 'mute of malice', he was pressed to death.

(7) In a letter to *The Times* Barrett referred with some bitterness to what was written concerning him and his activities by those whom he termed 'gentlemen of the type', i.e. journalists.

(8) It seems to me that there is a slight possibility that Summers' 'Cambridge man' was in fact an 'Oxford man' and that the occult tradition reported by Summers had become muddled. My belief in this possibility is based on the fact that a surviving early nineteenth century occult manuscript largely written in various of the magical alphabets contained in *The Magus* has an Oxford provenance. The manuscript (which also contains, written in ordinary English handwriting, a lengthy invocation which seem to belong to the same family as that contained in Barrett's instructions on crystal gazing) is rather splendidly bound in red with gold-stamped seals of the planets upon it. Inside the front cover is the bookplate of Henry Mansel (1820-71), an Oxford don with a strong interest in Gnosticism who eventually became Dean of St Paul's. While it is extremely unlikely, although not absolutely impossible, that Mansel was associated at any time of his life with a magical school derived from Francis Barrett it would be interesting to know both how and why he acquired it.

(9) The fact that in the Marriage Register Barrett was simply described as 'gentleman' does not necessarily mean that he had no occupation. By 1800 the description was being used of a great many men who were neither of independent means nor armigerous.

(10) To be more precise the signature as closely resembles known signatures of Barrett as the latter resemble one another. There are, of course, only very slight variations between them.

(11) The probability of the anvil having been purchased for

Chapter One

alchemical use is indicated by Barrett's remark that the lady's physique was 'very fit for the manual practice of handling iron, and working *other metallic experiments*' (my italics).

(12) See, however, Appendix B.

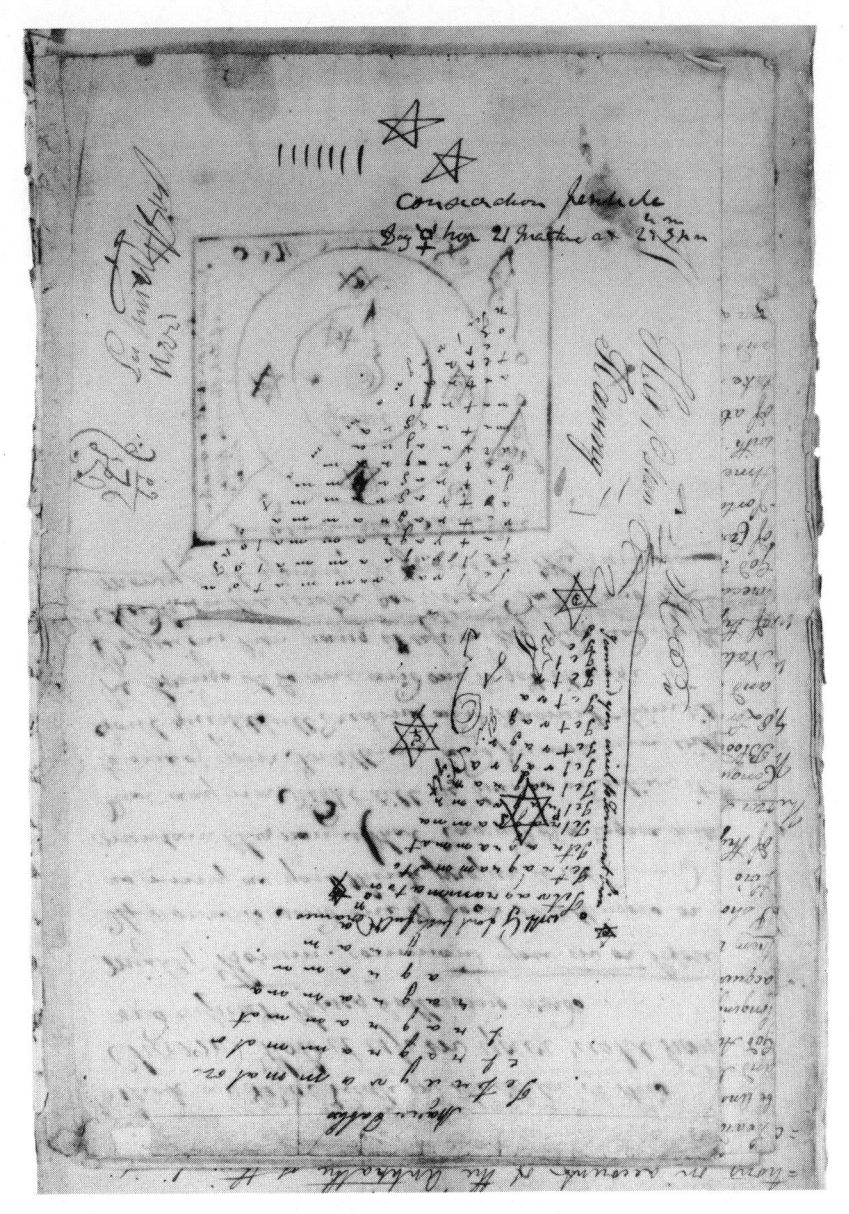

A page of Francis Barrett's script of the type employed by him when he was writing in great haste—usually almost illegible and frequently incorporating eccentric grammatical structures, orthography, and punctuation.

Chapter One

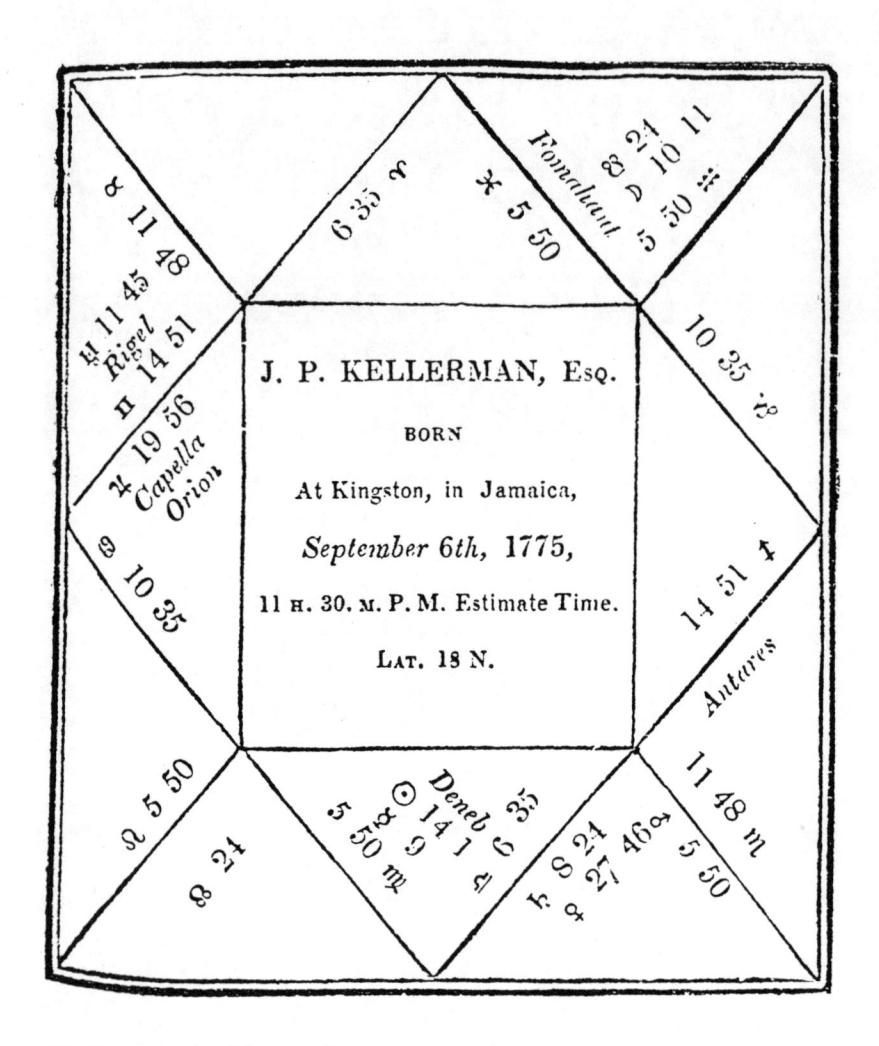

The horoscope of J. P. Kellerman as cast by the astrologer, geomancer and ritual magician Robert Cross Smith (1795-1832), the first of the many astrologers who have employed the pseudonym of 'Raphael'. It is possible that Kellerman, who may well have been a paranoid schizophrenic, was the real compiler of the Lives of the Alchymistical Philosophers *so often attributed to Francis Barrett.*

Chapter Two
The Sorcerer's Apprentice

MY ignorance of Francis Barrett's life after 1802 extends to the date of his death and its circumstances. It has been suggested to me that it took place in the United States, but I know of no hard evidence for this, although research being currently carried out by others—notably Mr Ron Heisler—may in due course provide such evidence. Two things would seem to be certain, however. Firstly, that the reference to 'the late Mr Barrett' in the note to the manuscript on crystal gazing quoted in the preceding chapter makes it apparent that Barrett predeceased his pupil John Parkins, who seems to have died at some time in the 1830s. For that note was written in the hand of John Parkins himself. And, secondly, that Francis Barrett or one or more of his associates kept in touch with at least some of those who had been linked with Barrett's magical school.

That John Parkins was associated with that school and not falsely claiming to be one of Barrett's pupils is shown by the fact that only a short time after Barrett wrote his instructional document on the subject of ritual crystal gazing key sections of it were copied by Parkins into his occult commonplace book, which survives in the library of the Wellcome Institute (WMS 3770). To me it would seem that there is little doubt that the crystal gazing manuscript was written by Barrett for the especial use

Chapter Two

of John Parkins.

Parkins, however, was involved in the occult subculture of late eighteenth century England at least five years before the publication of *The Magus*, for on page seventeen of his *Book of Miracles*...(1817) he casually observed:

> ...the late Dr Sibly, had both Saturn and Mars located in the seventh house in his nativity, and the consequence was this; he had two or three wives, but could not live with any of them. No person could have imagined or thought this to be the case, neither from his common conversation, address, accomplishment, or his company; yet, that unfortunate gentleman during the time that I was at his house in Upper Titchfield Street, London, in the year 1796, he was then living in a state of separation from his wife, whom I never saw all the while I was in town....

While there is a certain ambiguity in this passage it is apparent from it that Parkins, subsequently a pupil of Francis Barrett, definitely knew Sibly and may have for some time resided with him in Upper Titchfield Street. I feel that this fact provides some evidence in favour of an occult tradition, with which I first became acquainted in the 1950s, that Barrett learned his magical crystal gazing techniques from Sibly.

A further point of interest is that Sibly's address in 1796, Upper Titchfield Street, now the northern part of Great Titchfield Street, was the next road to Norton Street, now Bolsover Street, and the gardens of the houses on the western side of Upper Titchfield Street met the gardens of the houses on the eastern side of Norton Street. In other words, 99 Norton Street, where Francis Barrett established his magical school in 1801, was in remarkably close proximity to the house in which Ebenezer Sibly was living in 1796 and in which he probably died in October 1799. This may be no more than an extraordinary coincidence, but there seems some possibility that Catherine Collier, the rated inhabitant of 99 Norton Street, and thus Barrett's landlady, was a pupil or associate of Sibly—if so it would explain her rather surprising tolerance of Barrett's occult activities.

Whatever the truth of the matter may have been, of one thing we can at least be sure—John Parkins was an associate of both Sibly and Barrett and it was from them that he learned many of the occult

The Sorcerer's Apprentice

techniques he employed for the benefit of those who sought his help at the 'Temple of Wisdom' he established at some time before 1810 at Little Gonerly, near Grantham.

According to the anonymous author of *Ecce Homo* (Grantham, 1819), a scurrilous attack on 'Doctor Parkins', this pupil of Barrett was practising as an astrologer, fortune teller and 'Water-Caster' well before 1810, in which year he was prosecuted at Grantham Quarter Sessions, presumably under the Witchcraft Act.

Although he was looked upon as an astrologer in a passage of his *Book of Miracles* Parkins seems to have made the specific claim that he was *not* an astrologer, for he informed his readers 'that it is not my business to calculate nativities, for I never did bring any of the directions up in any person's nativity whatsoever, because it is of no use to burden or afflict the mind of any person whatsoever....'

By this Parkins meant no more than that he had never calculated primary directions in relation to the horoscope of a particular person. I do not doubt this—if only because I am reasonably sure that he lacked the knowledge of the fairly advanced mathematical techniques which are involved in such calculations. On the other hand there is no doubt that he was an astrologer in the ordinary sense of the word. Some horary figures (i.e, charts showing the position of the sun, moon and planets in the zodiac at the exact moment a question is asked of a soothsayer) drawn up by Parkins survive and his occult commonplace book contains an ingenious device of what would seem to have been his own invention for very quickly calculating the astrological aspects between the sun, moon and planets. So the author of *Ecce Homo* was justified in describing Parkins as an astrologer. He was also correct in describing him as a fortune teller and a 'Water-Caster'.

A Water-Caster was a healer, by the mid-eighteenth century almost invariably one without medical qualifications, of the sort vulgarly referred to as 'a piss prophet'—in other words a man who made diagnoses and prescribed remedies for his patients on the basis of the physical appearance of their urine.

It can be established that Parkins used such techniques from an examination of his commonplace book, for it contains a carefully compiled page index of the various references to the medical significance of the external appearance of urine to be found in a book Parkins referred

Chapter Two

to as 'Great Salmon'. There is also at least one reference in the commonplace book to 'Little Salmon'.

Both 'Great' and 'Little Salmon' were works on the subjects of astrological, herbal and alchemical medicine by William Salmon (1644-1713), a friend of Henry Coley, the adopted son of the astrologer William Lilly. Significantly, admirers of Salmon's and Coley's writings included both Sibly and Barrett, the latter specifically recommending (in a note on page 175 of Book 1 of *The Magus*) the study of '...Coley, his book, called Clavis Astrologiae Elimata, or his key new filed—Salmon's *Soul of Astrology....*'

Parkins' interest in fortune telling was made apparent in his *Universal Fortune-Teller* (1810), a book which its author described as an infallible guide to the secret and hidden decrees of fate and which contained sections dealing with such subjects as cartomancy, physiognomy, palmistry and even geomancy—'divination by earth'[1].

The inclusion of the last named is of some interest, for it demonstrates that there had been a continuing geomantic tradition in late Georgian England and that the use of geomancy by 'Raphael', G. W. Graham and other occultists associated with the magazine *The Straggling Astrologer* (June-October 1824) was not, as has been generally assumed, an artificial revival of an art of which the very existence had almost been forgotten.[2]

Parkins dealt with geomancy only very briefly in his *Universal Fortune-Teller*. He informed his readers that:

> This most wonderful art is received in a spiritual sublime virtue, and all artists and rosie crucians have demonstrated this to be twofold; the one whereof consisteth in religion and ceremonies, and therefore have the projecting of this art to be made with signs upon paper. Rosie Crucians also judge the hand of the projector to be most powerfully moved and directed by the ideas or genii or spiritual beings, when they ascend and descend in their respective regions...

> ...They then proceeded according to art to set the figure: In the first place, they made sixteen lines of points with the pen, thinking most anxiously and seriously on their said question in hand, the whole of the time.

Now having made these said sixteen lines of points, they did not count the numbers of points in each line as they made them, but in this they must fall just as it happens, which was called a Geomantic lot: afterwards they joined them together, leaving the odd points at each end, and from this they made out their first four figures, and proceeded in the manner and form shewn and proved in my said Holy Temple of Wisdom.

These details of how geomancy was (and still is) practised were expressed in language so vague that it might be thought that Parkins was only slightly acquainted with the techniques of that divinatory art. This was not so; various figures in his commonplace book show that he was an accomplished practitioner of astrogeomancy.

Parkins' vague instructions reproduced above were followed by a wretchedly printed table which he called '...the Names of the SEVEN RULERS of the EARTH, and also the NAMES of their TWELVE ANGELS with their SIXTEEN FIGURES'. The table does, in fact, include a good deal more than this. It shows the sixteen figures of geomancy, with their names in both Latin and English translation. Each figure is attributed to either one or two of the seven planets of traditional astrology and the names and sigils of both the spirits and the Angels of these planets are given. In addition each geomantic figure is attributed to one of the 'elements' of Fire, Air, Earth and Water and twelve of them are attributed to the signs of the zodiac. The elemental attributions are derived (as might be expected) from the obvious source, Cornelius Agrippa; the zodiacal attributions are not—nor, indeed, do they correspond with any of the various systems of attributing the signs of the zodiac to the sixteen geomantic figures which were in vogue during the Middle Ages and the Renaissance.

They do, however, correspond exactly with the zodiacal attributions as they were taught in the manuscript instructions regarding geomancy which were circulated after 1890 in the Hermetic Order of the Golden Dawn.[3] Presumably whoever compiled those instructions was drawing upon the same geomantic tradition, oral or written, as that within which Parkins was working eighty years before.

This is, to say the least, very odd. In a personal communication Mr Stephen Skinner, an authority on the history of geomancy, has suggested to me a possible (and plausible) explanation.

Chapter Two

The Golden Dawn manuscript on geomancy was, so Mr Skinner suggests (on the basis of internal evidence) compiled very largely from the information given in John Heydon's books *Theomagia* (3 vols., London 1662-64) and *El Havareuna* (London 1665).[4] While it is most unlikely that Parkins owned copies of either of these works, already exceptionally rare by 1810, it is possible that he learned his geomancy from someone who did own one or both of them. This hypothetical someone *could* have been Ebenezer Sibly, whose medical activities seem to have shown a possible indebtedness to the 'Rosicrucian medicine' practised by Heydon.

It may be that a full transcription of Parkins' commonplace book would reveal the exact truth about the source of the astrogeomantic system he employed; unfortunately much of that book is written in an archaic form of shorthand to which the key is known but which I can only read with extreme slowness and great difficulty. Nevertheless I have managed to read one very short extract which seems to be concerned with a talisman of Venus and the Moon and 'Lv Lds'—which I suggest is a contraction of 'Love of Ladies'. Perhaps large parts of the shorthand passages are concerned with similar sexual matters involving Parkins and/or his clients. If this was the case it would confirm various stories concerning Parkins' supposed attempts to seduce his female clients told by the anonymous author of *Ecce Homo*—that, for example, he refused to see a young strawbonnet maker except by herself, and that when she did come without a companion Parkins first asked her to undress, purportedly in order to enable him to examine certain marks on her body, and then demanded sexual intercourse.

It would be unsafe to accept this or any other story told by the author of *Ecce Homo*, who clearly wished to present Parkins as a man who was both sinister and absurd, without some confirmatory evidence. For at least one tale told by this anonymous author was clearly apocryphal.

According to this story a small farmer visited Parkins' 'Temple of Wisdom' with the object of consulting him on the subject of a cow which had disappeared, presumably because it had strayed or been stolen. Parkins was not at home so the farmer decided to await the magician's return. While waiting he found an urgent need to empty his bowels and, for some unexplained reason, chose to use the step of

The Sorcerer's Apprentice

Parkins' home as an improvised privy. When Parkins eventually returned home, so the story went on, and observed the mound of ordure on his step he was furiously angry and began to tell the waiting farmer what he, Parkins, would do to the culprit if he only knew that person's identity. To which the farmer supposedly replied that if Parkins didn't know who had polluted his steps he would certainly be unable to find a missing cow.

Almost exactly the same story was told in the seventeenth century concerning the astrologer William Lilly. It was probably old even then—clearly the author of *Ecce Homo* was prepared to repeat as fact any tale which would help to discredit Parkins.

However there is some confirmatory evidence of the claim made in *Ecce Homo* that Parkins, who claimed to be a loyal son of the Church of England, had once been a member of a dissenting congregation from which he had been expelled for 'drunkenness and hypocrisy'. For Parkins' books are loaded with scriptural quotations and references of the sort familiarly found in pamphlets written at that time by those to whom Cobbett rudely referred as 'canting Methodists'. That Parkins had at one time been a member of some Methodist body is also suggested by the fact that in one of his books he quoted from one of Wesley's hymns. As Wesley was a believer in the reality of witchcraft and regarded all forms of divination as works of the Devil I am forced to accept that if, as seems likely, Parkins had been a Methodist, his supposed expulsion for hypocrisy was well justified.

Parkins certainly practised horary astrology, geomancy, crystal gazing and unorthodox medicine—in relation to the latter, however, it is perhaps worth saying that his patients probably fared better under his ministrations than they would have done under those of his medically qualified rivals. Parkins was a herbalist—he produced a revised version of Nicholas Culpeper's herbal—and his remedies would certainly have done his clients little harm and possibly some good. Orthodox physicians and apothecaries of the time, however, still relied largely upon bloodletting and the administration of powerful and dangerous drugs such as opium and various mercurial derivatives; notably calomel.

Parkins had two other sources of income. For sums varying between twenty and thirty guineas he sold copies of a manuscript on the subject of ceremonial magic (presumably one compiled by himself

Chapter Two

from *The Magus* and other sources) and he also manufactured and sold talismans, which he termed 'holy consecrated lamens'.

He advertised these latter in short books which were sold, on a generous commission, by chapmen and pedlars. The following case histories from Parkins' *Book of Miracles* illustrate the extravagant claims he made for these articles:

> A certain tradesman, of the parish of Marston, came to my house on the fifth day of April, 1816, full of tears, he being in great grief, sorrow and affliction, who then informed me that his dearly beloved wife had run away with a tailor who was also a married man: this unhappy miserable deponent, most earnestly requested of me to let him have one of our holy consecrated Lamens, in order to oblige her to return to the arms of her most affectionate husband; but I was in a better disposition to have sent her two or three hundred miles another way, for reasons best known to myself; however, at length, after much persuasion, he prevailed upon me to put him in possession of this most valuable article, for which he paid me one guinea; which presently brought both these adulterous fugitives home again, as all the inhabitants of Marston can fully prove and testify; and I am informed by report, that they now live more happily together than ever they did before that time... another man came to me out of the country, and told me that his wife had gone away, and had eloped with a travelling bookseller; he said he wished to have her again, because 'she was such a very pretty creature', about twenty years younger than him, so I also sold him one of these articles, with a charge not to destroy the same, by which means, she was also soon obliged to return home again; but, when he found the Lamen had done its work, he destroyed the same, and the consequence was, she soon left him again, and I suppose his friends advised him to give himself no more trouble about her.

It is clear from these and other cases recorded by Parkins in both his printed works and his commonplace book that most of his clientele were concerned with matters that were traditionally the concern of the 'Cunning Man' or the 'Wise Woman'—but Parkins was something very

The Sorcerer's Apprentice

different from these traditional figures of English village life.

Of humble origins (his brother seems to have been a local village blacksmith) he was both a competent writer and an occultist who believed in that which he taught and practised. His 'Lamens', which the author of *Ecce Homo* denounced as mere pieces of rag scrawled with meaningless symbols, were carefully consecrated planetary talismans. This is made clear by entries in the commonplace book. This contains, for example, the elaborate tables of the planetary 'hours' needed by magicians if they are to consecrate such talismans at the appropriate time.

I have put the word 'hours' in inverted commas because, save at the equator, the planetary hours employed by magicians are only sixty minutes long on two days of each year. Almost equally confusingly the 'day' of Parkins and other talismanic magicians ran (and runs) from sunrise to sunrise—so that for the purposes of making talismans Friday, for example, commences at sunrise on that day and continues until sunrise on the Saturday. The 'magical Friday' is divided into a day of twelve 'hours', lasting from sunrise to sunset on a Friday and a night of twelve 'hours' lasting from Friday sunset until Saturday sunrise.

The length, in ordinary time, of the 'magical hours' of the day was and is calculated by dividing the sixty minute conventional hours between sunrise and sunset by twelve; a similar calculation is made for the hours of darkness. This means that at the latitude at which Parkins was consecrating his 'Lamens' a planetary 'hour' of the time between sunrise and sunset can vary in length from about forty minutes at the winter solstice to about one hour twenty-three minutes on midsummer day. A similar situation obtains for the period between sunset and sunrise, although in the case of these night 'hours' they are longest at the winter solstice. In his commonplace book Parkins not only wrote out a table of the planetary hours (giving such information as that the first hour of Friday is attributed to Venus and the first hour of Wednesday to Mercury) but an elaborate 'talismanic ready reckoner' which enabled him to calculate the exact length of a planetary 'hour' by day or night at different times of the year.

This demonstrates, as I have said, that Parkins was no mere 'Cunning Man'. Neither was he the charlatan portrayed by the author of *Ecce Homo*; he may have been greedy for money, but he was a

Chapter Two

conscientious manufacturer of talismans—it is clear from Parkins' commonplace book that this boastful quack doctor, who was accustomed to describe himself in print as the 'Grand Ambassador of Heaven' and to refer to his house as 'the Temple of Wisdom', was working in what was essentially the same tradition of astrological magic as such seventeenth century intellectuals as Campanella.

And yet Parkins unquestionably acted as the local 'Cunning Man' in the Grantham area—paradoxically he was an intellectual magician most of whose clients were drawn from the rural poor. This seems to me very curious; one cannot envisage either Ebenezer Sibly or Francis Barrett setting up as a village wizard and endeavouring to find the whereabouts of missing cows and it is surprising that a man who was associated with both of them should have done so.

A possible explanation for the curious ambivalence detectable in Parkins' activities is suggested to me by certain evidence that the (moderately) probable years of Parkins' birth were 1763, 1764 and 1765. If he was born in one of these years he would have been about thirty-two years old when he was staying with Sibly and some five years older when he became Barrett's pupil. It is unlikely, however, that he was an occult tyro at what was then considered a rather advanced age. While I know of no evidence of Parkins' occult activities before 1796 I surmise that he was *already* a village sorcerer/diviner, practising the traditional techniques of 'white witchcraft', well before he met Sibly, perhaps as the result of writing to him after he had read one of his books.

The last entry in Parkins' commonplace book, a draft of a new boasting circular concerning his 'holy consecrated Lamens', was made in the summer of 1829. It is to be presumed that he died not many years afterwards, leaving no pupils or successors behind him.

Oddly enough, however, his views on herbalism and herbal medicine still seem to have had their admirers in the North Wales of the 1860s and to have exerted some influence on Welsh-speaking herbalists of the time. This influence may have owed something to the Welsh connections of Francis Barrett.

It is known that in 1802 Barrett publicised his proposed balloon ascent at Swansea throughout the length and breadth of Wales: in the words of one contemporary observer he 'plastered the entire Principality' with leaflets. This demonstrates that he had contacts with North as well as South Wales. In 1815-18 a Caernarvon herbalist and botanist named David Thomas Jones published a Welsh version of Culpeper's Herbal; although the title page of the first edition of Jones' herbal does not say so it would seem that the English text used by Jones was that of Parkins' revised version of Culpeper, not that of the seventeenth century original. Interestingly enough the title page of a second and enlarged edition of Jones' book, which the British Library cataloguer has tentatively dated as '1862?' makes it clear that it includes material by 'Doctor Parkins'.

Unfortunately neither I nor, rather less expectedly, the National Library of Wales have been able to discover any biographical details concerning David Thomas Jones—even his dates of birth and death. It does seem possible, however, that he was the 'Doctor Jones' whom, as described in the preceding chapter, Barrett saw carry out the experiment on the corpse of a murdered man and, while Jones is an exceptionally common Welsh name, it is not beyond surmise that 'Doctor Jones' was a relation of the Grace Jones who was probably the mother of the author of *The Magus*.

Besides the existence in Caernarvon of a herbalist who was an admirer, perhaps even an associate, of Francis Barrett's enthusiastic disciple John Parkins there is a further possible link between *The Magus* and Caernarvon.

With the exception of the frontispiece of *The Magus*, which, as explained in the preceding chapter, was drawn and engraved by Daniel Orme all the illustrations in *The Magus* were drawn by Barrett himself and very competently engraved by someone who signed himself 'R. Griffith'. Somewhat desultory research carried out by me has failed to trace any other engravings by this 'R. Griffith', nor have I been able to trace any biographical information concerning him.

However at the time *The Magus* was published an extremely competent and well-travelled engraver, renowned for his depictions of scenery and people, was at work in Caernarvon. The man in question was Moses Griffith—and the lettering in some of his productions seems to my untutored eye to show similarities to that which features in the plates contained in *The Magus*.

Could 'R. Griffith' be in reality Moses Griffith, who had adopted the initial 'R' as he did not wish to be openly associated with such an eccentric production as *The Magus*? And could it be that Moses

Chapter Two

Griffith—or 'R. Griffith' if he was a different person—was a relation of the linen draper, Mr Griffith, with whom Barrett and his family resided during their stay in Swansea in 1802? Further research may in time enable these and other questions regarding the Welsh connections of Barrett and (possibly) Parkins to be answered.

The occult writings and the activities, magical and otherwise, of both Francis Barrett and John Parkins illustrate the fact that in the period 1800-1830 English occultism and occultists existed in a curious transitional period between the ossified esoteric tradition of eighteenth century Europe and the syncretistic ritual magic, influenced by non-European cultures, which developed in the years between, very roughly, 1830 and 1890.

On the one hand both Barrett and Parkins were traditionalists in their religious and magical beliefs. Both seem to have almost unthinkingly accepted the truth of orthodox Christian teachings—*The Magus* is full of Trinitarian formulae (as is the Barrett manuscript dealing with crystal gazing) and Parkins publicly expressed his loyalty to the Church of England. Both uncritically accepted the truth of the theories which underlay the magic they practised. Both had a belief in the efficacy of the traditional techniques they used—Parkins boasted that he had 'the whole Army of Heaven' at his command. Barrett did not go quite so far, but he claimed in print that he possessed the ability to produce thunderstorms by uttering mystic words.

And yet both men were clearly conscious that they were living in a rapidly changing world. For Barrett, with his ballooning endeavours, was operating on the frontiers of the technology of his own time while Parkins made full use of the power of cheap printing, with travelling booksellers selling his books, containing advertisements for his products, at low prices over a very wide area of England and, very probably, Wales.

A similar combination of old and new can be detected in the activities of other occultists of the 1820s, notably those concerned with the magazine *The Straggling Astrologer*. They were believers in ancient occult techniques, such as geomancy, astrology and talismanic magic—but they were also fascinated by recent discoveries both scientific and historical. By ballooning, for example, and the new information about Egypt which had reached Europe as a result of Napoleon's invasion and

The Sorcerer's Apprentice

the short French occupation of that country.

NOTES

(1) Geomancy seems to have been incorporated into the western divinatory *corpus* in the twelfth or thirteenth century and to have been derived, like several divinatory techniques widely employed in sub-Saharan Africa, from Arab sand divining. In this connection see Stephen Skinner's *Terrestrial Astrology* (London, 1980).

(2) For a detailed description of one of Raphael's geomantic divinations see Skinner *op. cit.*

(3) These were reproduced, although not in complete form, in the late F. I. Regardie's *Golden Dawn* (4 Vols. Minnesota 1937-1940). The missing portions were included by Crowley in the so-called *Treatise on Geomancy* to be found in The Equinox Vol. I No.I.

(4) I believe it to have been from one or more of Heydon's books that the Golden Dawn technique of obtaining quick geomantic answers from a 'Judge' and two 'Witnesses' was derived. Certainly it was from Heydon that the Golden Dawn leadership derived their employment of the sigils of Bartzabel and other spirits for geomantic purposes.

Appendix A

Barrett's Hitherto Unpublished Skrying Manuscript

WHOEVER attempts the invocation of Spirits by a Chrystal let him pay due attention to what is under written which was wrote at the especial desire of a Friend[1] whom I believe to be a sincere and true searcher into the Mysterious operations of Natural and Spiritual Magic.

The Chrystal that is sent with this (sic) few pages of Mss was consecrate by me, and made for my own particular use, and was shortly after borrowed by a Lady Aunt to a Disciple of mine, who had conceived a particular desire to have the use of it for a few weeks, in the space of which time she had two particular Visions, which satisfied her of the efficacy of Magic, or the possibility of Spirits appearing by this Mode of Invocation—having been favour'd (sic) with a sight of Spiritual Agents she returned it to me again.

These Visions were seen in the Chrystal at two several times, the first was on Wednesday after Midnight Noct.[Sol] Hor:[Mercury] viz. one o'clock on Thursday Morning.[2]

  Francis Barrett

  NB.—Here follows the Rites or Ceremonies Magical to be observed in all operations by the Chrystal or Circle. --
Rules

  Before any Man begins to use the Agency of Spirits he should first

Appendix A

examine himself to be assured whether he is qualified for so sublime and heavenly a Gift.

He must ask himself the following Questions. viz. To What purpose do I determine to consult and draw Spirits (whose Nature I know nothing at all about) to myself?

Is it for the glory of God and good of my Neighbour?

Or is it to enrich myself with monies and worldly Treasures, with vain glory and fame, to get a name amongst Men?—Or is it to *Know* seeing there are in this (*Enlightened*) Age so many who are ignobly ignorant, and who neither know/ nor wish to know anything besides *Eating and Drinking*?

If my friend your aim is *knowledge* / God give thee increase of Wisdom for if a man was born on a Dunghill (or in a *Manger*) If he desires to *know, that Man* is worth a *Million of Men* who carry fine cloaks on their Back and their *Heads* in their pocket. There is *nothing better* for a Man in a humble or high Sphere than Wisdom—how is it to be obtained; by seeking—by loving God—by fearing him—by endeavouring to mend our Heart—by loving the outcast of Mankind (*the poor*) *the humble*—*the Needy*—the afflicted—the Unfortunate! Love one another as I have loved you was (sic) the words of the blessed Redeemer of our *Souls*. how was this—what is Christianity? Where is its Glory? is it in the practise do we love one another? *We do* that desire wisdom we love one another therefore meer Christianity is deficient as it is practised—but Philosophy enforces us to follow the precepts of Christ which is (sic) seek first the Kingdom of God and all the rest you *shall* have --

When a Man thoroughly enters into himself he shall find 1st that he is entirely deficient without the aid of God and the holy spirit and with out a sole and firm dependance upon him he can never bring any wonderful thing to pass—although Necromancers affirm they can do Miracles (*so they think*). The Devil having a certain limited power can infuse himself into the souls of Men and being joined thereto can work many (seeming) wonderful effects—but they are mere illusions, nor truth cannot belong to them—Therefore it is better that a Man had never been born than that he should be inveigled by an Evil Spirit.

Therefore desire not to see any Spirit whatever *whether good or evil* but desire to see and converse with a good spirit either by Chrystal and Dream, or by inspiration and desire that you may be inform'd by the

Spirit what is best for thee to pursue whether Physick (or healing) or teaching others/ or *Metallurgy*—or *Herbs*, or *Prophecy* (which is the greatest) or anything else which might please God to call thee to for *every* Man hath his appointed end in this Globe of destruction--

My Friend seek to know how to help thy afflicted fellow Creatures in that (*I presume*) thou shalt please the (*Father*) and follow the precepts of the Son.[3]

I have observed your constancy and attention if you will be my / Disciple/ or Scholar/ signify the same by letter and I will try thee whether thou art fit—and if so I will initiate thee into the highest Mysteries of the Rosycrucian Discipline—but it will be necessary for you to come to London where I am to take the *Oath. This at a future time when thou art more practised in this art.*[4]

If you prove yourself unworthy after that sacred Oath is taken there is nothing but the Miraculous Mercy of the Eternal Wisdom can save thy Soul from Eternal perdition.

I would advise you that all worldliness must be done away neither family, nor Friends, nor Foes, nor any other consideration must amuse (sic) you from your Duty, which is principally the true adoration of the most high God, and to study how to do your duty in, this Vale of Misery—both towards God and your Neighbours.

These things being premised when you would use the Chrystal see that you touch no Animal Food for 24 hours nor drink no strong liquors whatever 'till the going down of the Sun and then only sufficient to clear nature and refresh thy Body.

Meditate Day and night on what you desire to know, have ready Pen and Ink—perfumes—the Virgin parchment—2 wax candles and 2 clean candle sticks, and a small earthen dish with lighted charcoal likewise the Pentacle of Solomon which you ought to draw out as describ'd in the Magus upon a piece of *Virgin Parchment* likewise the Name *Tetragrammaton* wrote upon a piece of Vellum fastened round your Forehead like a *wreath*.

Have ready a small new phial filled with clear Oil—olive with which you must anoint your eyelids and palms of both hands—and when all is ready make a small cross upon the flat side of the Chrystal where the Characters are and turn the convex side towards thy face—let it be placed between the two lights—but first all must be consecrated as it is

Appendix A

deliver'd in the *Magus*, therefore it would be needless to repeat them here--

You may omit the table on which the/chrystal is placed mentioned in the *Magus* with the wand which I never use—but instead sett the instruments upon the holy Bible saying

Consecration of the
Place whereon the
Bible and Chrystal is sett,

In the name of the Holy and Blessed Trinity—I consecrate this Table by virtue of the holy Bible wherein is contained the word of the Eternal Wisdom and by the holy Tables of the *Law* given unto Moses upon Mount Sinai—so that no Evil thing—may Enter hereon to die hurt or prejudice of any one—Bless O Lord all these instruments and experiments For the sake of thy Son Jesus Christ our Lord Amen.

* Here follows the *Call* or Invocation serving for any Spirit according to the *Day and Hour and Planet Ruling*

In the name of God the Father—God the Son—God the holy Ghost I conjure thee thou Spirit (———) By him Who spoke the word and it was done, Who is the beginning and the end—The First and the last, and by the Creation of the World, and by the last judgement that thou (———) appear here to me visible in this Chrystal, and by virtue of the holy bible on which it is placed that thou shalt give me true answers concerning those things which I may desire to know and be informed of and truly to instruct and to show us our desire without any guile or craft—this I do conjure thee quickly to do by virtue of him who shall come to judge the quick and the dead and the World by Fire Amen.--

Also I do conjure and exorcise thee (———) by the Sacrament of Christ's Body—By his Miracles—By the Sea—by the *Earth*, and by all things above and under the Earth and by their Virtues—by the seven planets—By the Seven Spirits which stand before the face of God and by the great Name of *God* Tetragrammaton, El-*Ousin* (sic) Agla—and by all the names of God holy and blessed and by all their Virtues—and by the Circumcision—Baptism—passion and Resurrection of our Lord Jesus Christ our Blessed Lord and Redeemer at whose Name the Devils do tremble—And by his Name *Emanuel* (sic) *Messias*, and by all the good and holy names of the blessed Trinity in Unity that thou Spirit whom I invoke quickly appear in this Chrystal visibly and with a plain and intelligible voice shew (sic) me those things which are proven for me to know; and answer and inform me of these things so I may propose to thee through our Lord and Saviour Jesus Christ Amen.

The Spirit will appear after having read the call fervently on thy Knees 7 times over.

Then being satisfied of what thou wouldst Know of the Spirit use this Dismissal or License for the Spirit to depart which thou shalt not detain above one planetary hour.

The License

God hath appointed thee a place, go in his name to wherever thou art familiar, Be ready to come when I call thee in his name to whom (sic) every Knee doth bow both of things in heaven and things in Earth and things under the Earth, I license thee to depart in the name of the *Father, Son* and Holy Ghost.

Here repeat the Prayer in the Magus returning thanks to God with any additional prayers or Psalms thou mayest think proper.

Note

Before you intend to work erect a figure of the Heavens so that the Spirit governing the Planet and let the Planet you would work under be in an Angle and strong and the [moon] increasing for all other observations refer to the Magus. In all your operations let not your own significator be under the Earth but in as fortunate a part of heaven as can be convenient.[5]

Let not the [moon] be combust when you work—Observe to be clean washed and linnen clean—Also let there be a new clean linnen cloth on the table under the Chrystal.[6]

Let your suffumigation be strong and plenty of it, and let all things be consecrated and blessed consecrate the Water with Salt and use the consecrations mentioned in the Magus.

(Note: *At this point Barrett's purely practical instruction to his pupil comes to an end and, in a different hand, presumably that of Doctor Parkins, is inserted a curious note.*[7] *There immediately follows, however,* **On Spiritual Vision,** *an essay by Barrett which clearly was considered*

Appendix A

by him to have both theoretical and practical implications for those who sought to be his disciples in the 'Rosycrucian discipline'.)

On Spiritual Vision

The Ancient Magi amongst their Philosophical researches into Nature and Magic discover'd a possibility of communicating with Celestial, Astral and inferior (?) Spirits, that is by *fasting* and *prayer* they received oracles from God, through the Medium of the Celestial spirits who received their instructions from the Blessed intelligences or 7 Spirits who constantly stand before the face of *Jehovah*—by these means they drew as it were from the Original Archetype of all things the knowledge of future Events and the prediction of the contingencies of *Human Affairs* and not only the Knowledge of Nature and natural things but likewise, they discover'd further that the 4 Elements had their invisible, as well as their visible inhabitants from the highest to the lowest i.e. from Heaven to Earth—Therefore they divided those legions into sundry classes—first they sett in order the nine quires of Angels—then followed the Spirits of the Fiery Region, then of the Airy Regions: of the Watery—Earthly of the Earth, which are not properly to be called Astral Spirits as these were more nearly assimilated to the Nature of Man and were found even to be subject to human affections and to solicit a kind of Copulation with Men, and women.

These different orders of Spirits Astral Elementary etc. are fully described in the book called the Magus therefore it is needless to be repeated here—My intent being to come directly to the forms and ways by which the wise ancients attracted those Spirits into communication, and which was accounted by them and all others no trifling, or easy operation, but the highest point of Human Wisdom and to which they gave the title of Magic, a name significant enough for such a scope of knowledge as enabled Men to know and converse not only with visible creatures, but with Invisible angels and spirits, and this they did by various forms, prayers, invocations, suffumigations, *Mirrors Glasses*, Circles and the like attended with abstinence from all carnal affairs and perturbations of the mind. But one method which was held in great repute was a mode of invocating Spirits by a *Chrystal* of which I intend principally to speak in this place.

But first it is necessary for me to explain to you they made use of these 4 instruments in the invocation of Spirits.

First you must consider that it is Law in *Natural* as well as in *Occult Philosophy* that no Spirit seeing that they are of an immaterial form, can manifest themselves to the human eye, without some medium, by which they can somehow or other Materialise their Spiritual and immortal Bodies nor can flesh and blood see but what is in of some sort substantial, and of its own nature for we cannot see fire without some material body, as *wood, flint, steel*, etc. etc. nor can we see the air unless it is colour'd, although we perceive it both hot and cold, yet still it remains invisible to sight, smell or touch unless it be moved and stirred up or perfumed or colour'd.

Therefore seeing that the Nature and operations of Spirits are so very different to those of Tangible Bodies hence arose the great difficulty of a Spirit manifesting itself to the human Organs, without some Medium to be used by him who would communicate with them— but it was discover'd that this inconvenience was in a great measure removed by using some certain things agreeable and sympathising with the nature of the Spirits, and nothing was found more adapted than *powerful* suffumigations, by the thick vapour and cloud produced by these it not only enabled the Spirits to clothe themselves with an artificial and temporary body by which they being insolved? Produced a certain visible appearance to the human Sight, *formed* out of the combination of the Elementary chaos produced by these suffumigations, and these perfumes served a twofold purpose first to render the operation more attractive as well as to spiritualise the operator, and excite his spirits, and make him more fit, for such an operation, he having been previously prepared by long fasting and abstinence from every gross and superfluous thing relative to the Flesh—for it is undoubtedly held, by all who know any thing of spiritual operations that at the time and minute of a Spirit's becoming visible it is such a shock to our frail natural Body—that a sickness and trembling falls upon a Man, almost like to Death, and by an indispensable Law of Providence, he is rapt up as it were into a delirious Ecstasy of Soul, and it requires every resolution, faith, and firmness of Soul, to stand firmly before such tremendous Visitors—I am now speaking chiefly of the operation by a circle.[8]

The other method of communicating which is by a Chrystal or a

Appendix A

Beryl, or a smooth shining steel Mirror, is not attended with such a violent conflict of Soul and Body—Although I deem a suffumigation as necessary in this, as the other; and this brings me to the subject on which you desired me to speak on which I will here for your full satisfaction sett down everything that is necessary to be done for the obtaining of a spiritual vision in the Chrystal which you may try whenever convenient, you having one by you already sett and consecrated.

And which hath already been used, to the conviction of the party which used it; accounts of which I have before given you.

But first I would advertise (sic) you that all *forms perfumes Papers Pentacles circles times hours incantations* etc, and the *Chrystal* itself will not be of any use whatsoever, without you can entirely abstract your mind, from every worldly affair for a Season, excite within yourself the supernatural powers[9] and firmly ground within yourself a strong and vehement Faith (which is the chief Key of this Art) and for 7 days at least fast and abstain from all heavy rich and strong drink; and take nothing from the rising until the going down of the [Sun] but bread and water—after Sunsett you may without inconvenience take some simple and light refreshments this being observed, with every morning making prayer for that which you desire in a quiet place free from Noise and bustle proceed on to the accomplishments of your purpose—without these observations nothing can be done either by a Christal (*sic*) or circle—Then having Elected a due and fit time and having all your materials ready, with the proper suffumigations charcoal fire in a new earthen dish proceed on, the morning you would to the work to pronounce the following prayer which I send you with these writings[10] which has been used already on a similar occasion, which when you have copied out you will please to send back to me again (*but in no hurry for it*).

You will repeat this prayer 7 times on the day on which you mean to invocate, and if you think proper every morning during the 7 days fasting and abstinence.

Now as you have in the *Magus* the directions of the Perfumes attributed to each planet under which you work I should conceive it unnecessary to mention them *again* here.

I would advise that this work might be done in some retired place at a distance from your house, rather than in your own chamber—But you may in this act as you please—I would only observe that the Spirits are sooner attracted to an unfrequented place than to appear in a house.

In the hour which you work read over the form of prayer I now send at the beginning then use the call I have sent before with the Chrystal, making use of any other prayers you may think fit—You ought not to think any thing of that kind to be done on this occasion a trouble. As many do who wish to gratify mere curiosity with some other person to put every Syllable into their mouths, and every instrument into their hands, without the least painstaking or search of themselves.

I can compare such, only to those who after a Philosopher has discover'd the transmutation of Metals from many wearied years of intense labour and study, shew me—shew me—that I may believe, and do the same—to such I answer knowledge and wisdom is gained with great labour intense study and pains taking; both of Body and Mind.

Your Chrystal being placed before you on the Table, and your *Fire Water Incense* Suffume and consecrated you must then use the invocation or call repeating the same 7 times.

Do not touch the Chrystal with your hands after placing it on the Table.

Have ready some clean white paper or Virgin parchment to write down the name of the Spirit, his *Planet* Sign and character which he may shew you.

Afterwards put what Questions you may wish to be informed of returning thanks to the Creator, Ask the Spt. at what Seasons and times it would be most eligible, and (or?) agreeable for him to come to you. And for what business his character is proper to be used for and on what occasions.

And ask him of all those things which seem agreeable to his Nature and office to communicate.

When this is done and an hour expired license him to depart and return thanks to God.

Keep the character and name of the Spirit by itself free from any prophane or polluted thing.

And thus far is the method of the invoking a Spirit by the Christal (*sic*) or Mirror or Berryl (*sic*) freely and without reserve communicated to you. Observe whatever your purpose, or end is by undertaking this Experiment of such kind or nature will be the Spirit, whom you shall

Appendix A

attract or draw to you.

Let your intentions be not from a desire of Money or Riches but to learn some Secret whereby you may assist your fellow Creatures.

Note, if you do not chance to succeed in this operation nevertheless do not despair but, try your work with a Spirit of another order as if you try the first time under [Jupiter] let your next work be under [Mars] or [Venus] or [Mercury] or the [Moon].

There has been no time of late fit for the operation of calling or invocating of Spirits.

And the success depends greatly upon doing the operation under that *Spirit* and *planet* who is ruler or governour of the part, or Region in which you may operate, likewise to consider, what dignity essential or accidental whether fortunate or unfortunate, likewise what affinity or agreement the Significator of the operator has with the ruler of that place—otherwise some working ignorant of these things have been snatch'd away in the very midst of their Incantations, on account of the Antipathy of their Significator with that ruler or prince[11]

Therefore every thing shou'd be as exactly suited as near agreement as can be, both in *time, nature of the Invocant,* place, suffumigation etc. to the nature of the planet and spirit who has the chief rule and (or) dominion over the part in which we are to work.

These things being duly observ'd'd I think if you are a Man permitted, or design'd to work in these Mysteries that you will not fail of the desired success with which I beg leave to conclude this present writing and am Sir

Your Friend etc.-F.B. May 5th. 1802.

In the day and hour [Mercury]

NOTES

(1) The 'friend' was, so it is to be presumed, John Parkins.

(2) Barrett was here using a most unusual method of indicating a planetary hour. 'Noct.[Sol]' means the night commencing at sunset on a Wednesday—the first hour of the night of each Wednesday being supposedly governed by the Sun. 'Hor.[Venus]' means either the second or the ninth hour after sunset on a Wednesday—both dedicated to Venus. In relation to the length of planetary 'hours' see my explanation

on earlier pages. It is worth adding that the time of a magical operation intended to be carried out by Barrett on February 27 1802 was given by him as 'noct,[Mercury] Hor.[Mars]'. February 27 1802 was a Saturday and the first planetary hour of each Saturday night is dedicated to Mercury. I conjecture that Barrett's curious convention of calling a night by the name of the planet ruling its first hour was a blind—most occultists would interpret [Mercury] as a Wednesday rather than a Saturday night.

(3) In the original the word Son is underlined thrice, presumably, for greater emphasis.

(4) This passage is confusingly lacking in proper punctuation. I am confident that when Barrett wrote 'it will be necessary for thee to come to London where I am to take the Oath', what he intended to say was '...for thee to come to London, where I am, to take the *Oath*'. In other words, Barrett was proposing to administer some oath of allegiance and/or secrecy to his pupil before initiating him into the mysteries of the 'Rosycrucian Discipline'.

(5) This paragraph is not easily understandable without some knowledge of the terminology of eighteenth century astrology. An individual's 'significator' was regarded as the planet ruling the astrological sign which was rising above the horizon (geocentrically considered) at the moment of that individual's birth. If, for example, Capricorn had been rising at the moment of a person's birth the 'significator' would have been taken as Saturn. Barrett was advising that no magical operation should be carried out by his pupil at a time when that pupil's significator was 'under the Earth', i.e. below the horizon, and thus in one of the first six houses of a horoscope. By 'let the Planet you would work under be in Angle and strong' was meant something like 'Let the Planet ruling the spirit you invoke be in the first, fourth, seventh or tenth houses of a horoscope you have drawn up for the time at which you plan to invoke; and let that Planet be both well aspected and in a zodiacal sign with which it is compatible'.

(6) 'Combust' was a term applied by eighteenth century astrologers to the moon or any planet when its zodiacal position was within a few degrees of that of the Sun.

(7) The note in question reads as follows:

The most noble Science of Divine Magic, which is the

Appendix A

highest Branches (sic) of Learning is regularly taught in all its parts by Dr. Parkins Pupil to the late

Little Gonerly   Mr. F. Barrett
near Grantham
Lincolnshire

(8) This whole paragraph is, I believe, of great importance in relation to Barrett's beliefs. It seems to indicate that he anticipated the theories about the *psychological* importance of perfumes and incense in magical rites which were independently developed in the twentieth century by such occultists as Aleister Crowley and Dion Fortune.

(9) Barrett seems to be describing the same technique as that which such initiates of the occult society known as the Hermetic Order of the Golden Dawn as W. B. Yeats and Aleister Crowley termed 'enflaming by prayer'—a phrase derived from a late classical text, *The Chaldean Oracles of Zoroaster.*

(10) The reference is, I think, to the prayer which occupies most of pages ten recto and verso of the manuscript. The prayer was used, or intended to be used, at the beginning of a rite for the invocation of a Saturnian and/or Martial spirit—or so I suppose from the fact that the 'perfumes' for the rite included sulphur, hellebore and euphorbium and that the operation was intended to take place in the planetary hour dedicated to Mars. The prayer reads as follows:

> Almighty and most merciful Lord God. I thy poor humble and unworthy Servant being an admirer of Wisdom and a Votary of Science and Student of Knowledge by the Creature (sic) desirous of true spiritual light although a Worm Subject to the Frailties Wickedness Temptations and Casualties of the Flesh. Grant O great Jehovah that I may this Night see by thy Divine Will and Wonderful Power those Spirituals that may inform me of those good and wholesome things for my Soul that may be beneficial to me in my Mortal and Corruptible (sic) state. Grant O most beneficent Being to me being desirous of holy things and Willing to Pursue the Paths of Knowledge and true Wisdom. O Lord I beseech thee to forgive my Sins and mercifully incline they heavenly Ear to my Petitions which I now with my whole Heart Soul and

Mind offer thee and beseech thee to take away the Cloud of Sensuality and dullness that I may clearly behold the Spirit I invoke this day this I earnestly pray thinking nothing better for a Man in this World than to be informed of things above Corruption and to enjoy the Sublime Benefit of seeing Spiritually and Conversing with thy blessed intelligences but this I know myself unworthy off (sic) as I am a fleshly Creature. But O God; as thy Son Jesus Christ saith 'Whatsoever ye ask that shall ye receive' so most mighty God I being One Man ask to receive divine illumination by the Ministry of thy Spirit who is a pure Spirit whom I do desire to see Openly and Fully to Converse with Him O God this day and Grant great Jehovah that I may be taught Wisdom by this said Spirit this day and that no evil Spirit whatsoever may have Power to come in the Name of the good Spirits and deceive me to the Ruin of my Souls health. O most mighty God I beseech thee to Pardon this my imbecility in thinking myself Capable of making myself heard but as I ask let me receive as mine intentions are. So let me be Answered. I know my own unworthiness O Lord great are my Sins and iniquity they are more than the Hairs upon my Head. But O Lord God Almighty if I have found any favour in thy sight, if my anxious longing after Knowledge and true Wisdom, if my anxious endeavours to acquire it, be pleasing to thee O thou Fountain of Life Light and Wisdom, then let one of thy Spirits descend and make known to me what Course I should pursue. O Almighty and merciful Jehovah I wish thro' the medium of a gross and earthly Body to exert that spark of thy divine Essence which I believe thou didst formerly breath into our Nostrils with the Breath of Life Enable me O God Almighty to Conquer those bad passions which every day rise in my heart. Let the Blood of Christ be an Atonement for my Sins and Grant that me O Lord who am a Disciple of Wisdom whose desire is to attain knowledge and to destroy those Seeds sown by our Human Nature. O God Grant I may be Rapt up in the Divine Vision of thy Holy spirit through Jesus Christ who Sacrificed precious and immortal Blood

Appendix A

upon the Cross Enable me O most high to immediately become a Servant of thy Will and also an instrument curing the Sick and the Diseased, of relieving the distressed fortifying the Afflicted. O (sic) doing all the Good that may be man Amen—O Lord Jesus Christ I earnestly beseech thee to intercede with the Father on my behalf. Be pleased O most merciful God Ruler of all things Visible and Invisible to grant my petitions and take not thy Holy spirit from me. But let Him descend this day and make known those things I desire through Jesus Christ our Lord Amen—

While I have no doubt that this prayer was composed by Barrett—its confusion could hardly have derived from any traditional source—it may well be that it was copied, somewhat inaccurately, by someone helping him with his correspondence. The handwriting seems slightly different from that he usually employed, even when writing in great haste, and the punctuation of the original goes beyond eccentricity; no commas were employed and full stops were scattered literally at random. For the sake of readers of this prayer I have therefore punctuated it in an attempt to convey what I believe to have been its original meaning.

(11) This paragraph clearly indicates the immense importance which Barrett attached to astrology in relation to ritual scrying; he seems to have been suggesting that if a city was ruled by a particular zodiacal sign the magus should not carry out invocations therein unless his significator, the planet ruling the ascendant of his nativity, was strong or exalted in that sign.

Appendix B
J. P. Kellerman and Late Georgian Alchemy

IT is generally assumed that alchemy in England was no longer a subject of serious study by circa 1780.
 This does not seem to have been the case. Throughout the reigns of Kings George III and IV (1760-1830) alchemical writings were the subject of intense interest to some mystics and a small minority of these appear to have carried out laboratory experimentation.
 Thus, for example, an Anglican mystic, the Rev. Richard Clarke (1720?-1802) wrote of alchemy in a letter dated February 20, 1779 that he knew:

> ...the science to be true, but content myself without searching for it. Though most searchers into that mystery think I possess it; as they cannot conceive how I could write in the line I do, without that knowledge. I believe I know the whole....

One who also believed he 'knew the whole' was J. P. Kellerman (1779-18??) a practising alchemist who could well have been the author of the *Lives of the Alchymistical Philosophers* so often attributed to Francis Barrett.
 Amongst Kellerman's admirers was the astrologer, geomancer

Appendix B

and ritual magician 'Raphael' who wrote of him that he was 'a gentleman of great accomplishments' and that he had often heard 'my friend Mr. V. speak in praise of his attainments'.

Raphael's comment was made in the course of a criticism of an account of Kellerman given by the publisher Sir Richard Phillips. This account—which Raphael denounced as ungentlemanly, unworthy, unphilosophical and written in a ludicrous style—is worthy of reproduction and reads as follows:

> It was four miles out of the road; but I thought a modern alchemist worthy of a visit, particularly as several inhabitants of Luton gravely assured me that he had succeeded in discovering the Philosopher's Stone, and also the Universal Solvent. The reports about him would have rendered it culpable not to have hazarded anything for a personal interview. I learnt that he had been a man of fashion and at one time largely concerned in adventures on the turf; but that for many years he had devoted himself to his pursuits; while, for some time past, he had been inaccessible and invisible to the world—the house being shut and barricaded, and the walls of his grounds protected by hurdles, with spring-guns so planted as to resist intrusion in every direction. Under these circumstances I had no encouragement to go to Lilley, but I thought that even the external inspection of such premises would repay me for the trouble. At Lilley, I inquired for his house, of various people, and they looked ominous; some smiled others shock their heads, and all appeared surprised at the approach of an apparent visitor to Mr Kellerman.
>
> The appearance of the premises did not belie vulgar reports. I could not help shuddering at seeing the high walls of respectable premises lined at the top with double tiers of hurdles; and on driving my chaise to the front of the house, I perceived the whole in a state of horrid dilapidation. Contrary however, to my expectations, I found a young man, who appeared to belong to the outbuildings, and he took charge of my card for his master, and went to the back of the house to deliver it. The front windows on the ground-floor

and the upper stories were entirely closed by inside shutters; much of the glass was broken, and the premises appeared altogether as if deserted. I was pleased at the words, 'My master will be happy to see you'; and in a minute the front door was opened and Mr. Kellerman presented himself. I lament that I have not the pencil of Hogarth, for a more original figure never was seen. He was about six feet high, and of athletic make; on his head was a white night-cap, and his dress consisted of a long great-coat once green, and he had a sort of jockey waistcoat with three tiers of pockets. His manner was extremely polite and graceful, but my attention was chiefly absorbed by his singular physiognomy. His complexion was deeply sallow; and his eyes large, black and rolling. He conducted me into a very large parlour, with a window looking backward; and having locked the door, and put the key in his pocket, he desired me to be seated on one of two large arm-chairs covered with sheepskins. The room was a realization of the well-known picture of Teniers' Alchemist. The floor was covered with retorts, crucibles, jars, bottles in various shapes, intermingled with old books piled upon each other, with a sufficient quantity of dust and cobwebs. Different shelves were filled in the same manner; and on one side stood his bed. In a corner, somewhat shaded from the light, I beheld two heads, white, with dark wigs on them; I entertained no doubt, therefore, that among other fancies, he was engaged in remaking the brazen speaking head of Roger Bacon and Albertus. Many persons might have felt alarmed at the peculiarity of my situation; but being accustomed to mingle with eccentric characters, and having no fear from any pretensions of the Black Art, I was infinitely gratified by all I saw.

Having stated the reports which I had heard, relative to his wonderful discoveries, I told him frankly that mine was a visit of curiosity; and stated that if what I had heard was matter of fact, the researches of the ancient chemists had been unjustly derided. He then gave me a history of his studies; mentioning some men whom I had happened to

Appendix B

know in London, who he alleged had assured him that they had made gold. That having in consequence examined the works of the ancient alchemists, and discovered the key which they had studiously concealed from the multitude, he had pursued their system under the influence of new lights; and after suffering numerous disappointments, owing to the ambiguity with which they described their processes, he had at length succeeded, and made gold; and could make as much more as he pleased, even to the extent of paying off the national debt in the coin of the realm.

I yielded to the declaration, expressed my satisfaction at so extraordinary a discovery, and asked him to oblige me so far, as to show me some of the precious metal he had made.

'Not so,' said he; 'I will show it to no one. I made Lord Liverpool the offer, that if he would introduce me to the King, I would show it to His Majesty; but Lord Liverpool insolently declined, on the ground that there was no precedent; and I am therefore determined that the secret shall die with me. It is true, in order to avenge myself of such contempt, I made a communication to the French ambassador, Prince Polignac, and offered to go to France, and transfer to the French Government the entire advantages of the discovery; but after deluding me, and shuffling for some time, I found it necessary to treat him with the same contempt as the others.'

I expressed my convictions in regard to the double dealing of men in office.

'O', said he, 'as to that, every court in Europe well knows that I have made the discovery; and they are all in confederacy against me lest, by giving it to any one, I should make that country master of all the rest; the world, Sir', he exclaimed with great emotion, 'is in my hands and my power.'

Satisfied with the announcement of the discovery of the philosopher's stone, I now inquired about the sublime alkahest, or universal solvent, and whether he had succeed in deciphering the enigmatic descriptions of the ancient writers on that most curious topic.

'Certainly', he replied; 'I succeeded in that several years ago'.

'Then', I proceeded, 'have you effected the other great desideratum—the fixing of mercury?'

'Than that process', said he, 'there is nothing more easy; at the same time it is proper I should inform you, that there are a class of impostors, who, mistaking the ancient writers, pretend it can be done by heat; but I can assure you it can only be effected by water.'

I then besought him to do me the favour to show me some of his fixed mercury; having once seen some which had been fixed by cold.

This proposition, however, he declined, because, he said, he had refused others. 'That you may, however, be satisfied that I have made great discoveries, here is a bottle of oil, which I have purified, and rendered as transparent as spring water. I was offered £10,000 for the discovery; but I am so neglected and so conspired against, that I am determined it and all my other discoveries shall die with me.'

I now inquired, whether he had been alarmed by the ignorance of the people in the country, so as to shut himself up in so unusual a manner.

'No', he replied; 'not on their account wholly. They are ignorant and insolent enough; but it was to protect myself against the Governments of Europe, who are determined to get possession of my secret by force. I have been', he exclaimed, 'twice fired at in one day through that window, and three times attempted to be poisoned. They believed I had written a book containing my secrets, and to get possession of this book has been their object. To baffle them, I burnt all that I had ever written, and I have so guarded the windows with spring-guns, and have such a collection of combustibles

Appendix B

in the range of bottles which stand at your elbow, that I could destroy a whole regiment of soldiers if sent against me.' He then related, that as a further protection he lived entirely in that room, and permitted no one to come into the house; while he had locked up every room except that with patent padlocks, and sealed key-holes.

It would be tedious and impossible to follow Mr. Kellerman through a conversation of two or three hours, in which he enlarged upon the merits of the ancient alchemists, and on the blunders and impertinent assumptions of the modern chemists, with whose writings and names it is fair to acknowledge he seemed well acquainted. He quoted the authorities of Roger and Lord Bacon, Paracelsus, Boyle, Boerhaave, Woolfe and others, to justify his pursuits. As to the term philosopher's stone, he alleged that it was a mere figure, to deceive the vulgar. He appeared, also, to give full credit to the silly story about Dee's assistant, Kelly, finding some of the powder of projection in the tomb of Roger Bacon of Glastonbury, by means of which, as it was said, Kelly for a length of time supported himself in princely splendour.

I inquired whether he had discovered the blacker than black of Apollonius Tyaneus; and this, he assured me, he had effected; it was itself the powder of projection for producing gold.

Amidst all this delusion and illusion on these subjects, Mr. Kellerman behaved in other respects with great propriety and politeness; and having unlocked the door, he took me to the doors of some of the other rooms, to show me how safely they were padlocked; and on taking leave, directed me in my course towards Bedford.

In a few minutes, I overtook a man; and on inquiring what the people thought of Mr. Kellerman, he told me that he had lived with him for seven years; that he was one of eight assistants whom he kept for the purpose of superintending his crucibles,—two at a time relieving each other every six hours; that he had exposed some preparations to intense heat

Late Georgian Alchemy

for many months at a time, but that all except one crucible had burst, and that he called on him to observe, that it contained the true 'blacker than black'. The man protested, however, that no gold had ever been made, and that no mercury had ever been fixed; for he was quite sure, that if he had made any discovery, he could not have concealed it from the assistants; while, on the contrary, they witnessed his severe disappointment in the termination of his most elaborate experiments.

On my telling the man that I had been in his room, he seemed much astonished at my boldness; for he assured me that he carried a loaded pistol in every one of his six waistcoat pockets. I learnt also from this man, that he has, or had, considerable property in Jamaica; that he has lived in the premises at Lilley about twenty-three years, and during fourteen of them pursued his alchemical researches with unremitting ardour; but for the last few years shut himself up as a close prisoner, and lived in the manner I have described.

Index

Abano, Peter de 18, 28
Agrippa, Cornelius 18, 28
Alchemy and the Occult 28
Andrade, Chevalier, 12

Bacon, Francis, 18
Barrett, Ann, 29
Barrett, Francis *junior*, 14, 31-32
Barrett, Grace, 14, 31, 49
Bellows, 15
Blood, human, 21-23
Books of the Beast, 19, 34
Brandy, 16
Bristol, 15
Cambridge, 25, 26
Catherine Street (Cavendish Square), 32
Chaldean Oracles, 64
Clarke, Rev. Richard, 68
Cobbett, William, 45
Coley, Henry, 42
Crowley, Aleister, 51, 64
Crystal Gazing, Ritual, 53-66
Culpeper, Nicholas, 45

d'Arch Smith, Timothy, 9, 17, 18, 19, 33, 34
Denley, John, 19-20, 34
Directions for the Invocation of Spirits, 26

Ecce Homo, 41, 44, 45, 48
Experimentorum...Liber, 18

Fortune, Dion, 64
Fourth Book of Occult Philosophy, 18

Garnerin M., 12
Geomancy, 42-44, 50, 51
George Inn (Swansea), 14 *et seq*
Golden Dawn, Hermetic Order of the, 43, 44, 51, 64
Gorn, Walter Old, 32
Graham, G. W., 42
Greenwich, attempted balloon ascent at, 10-14, 24, 29
Griffith Mr, 14, 50
Griffith, Moses, 49-50
Griffith, R., 49-50
Gum varnish, elastic, 16

Harmony of the World, 18
Heisler, Ron, 25, 26, 33, 39
Helmont, J. B. van, 21
Heptameron, The, 18
Heydon, John, 18, 44
Hockley, Frederick, 19
Hours, Planetary, 47, 62-63

Jones, David Thomas, 49
Jones, Dr, 22, 29, 49
Jones, Grace--see Barrett, Grace

Kellerman, J. P., 67-73

Lamens--see Talismans
Lilly, William, 42, 45
Lives of Alchemical Philosophers, 33-34, 67
Lytton, Bulwer, 20

Madoc, Mr, 13
Magical Elements, The--see *Heptamenon, The*
Magus, The, 9, 10, 17-25, 27, 28, 29, 32, 33, 34, 40, 42, 46, 49-50
Miracles..., Book of, 40, 41, 46
Montgolfiers (hot air balloons), 14-15

Neath, 15
New Atlantis, 18
Norcott, Johane, 22-23
Norton Street, 24, 40

Orme, Daniel, 27

Parkins, 'Dr' John, 26, 39-50, 62
Phillips, Sir Richard, 68
Prince's Street (Cavendish Square), 32, 33

'Raphael', 42, 51, 68
Rise and Origin of Common Salt, The--see Welling, Georg von
Rosicrucianism, 10, 17, 42, 55, 63
Royal Artillery, 11

Salmon, William, 42
'Sepharial'--see Gorn, Walter Old
Sibley, Ebenezer, 40, 42, 44
Skinner, Stephen, 43-44, 51

Southey, Robert, 9-10, 34
Sowden, Captain, 14
Spry, Edward 'Dr', 29-30
Straggling Astrologer, The, 42, 50
Summers, Montague, 25
Talismans, 46, 48

Umbrellas, 15
Universal Fortune-Teller, 42-43

Vitriol, Oil of (Sulphuric acid), 11, 15, 16

Waite, A. E., 33
Welling, Georg von, 27, 28
Wesley, John, 45

Yeats, W. B., 64

Zanoni, 20

Other Mandrake Titles of Interest

Jan Fries's *Visual Magick*
1992 136pp 1869928-180 £6.99 pbk
A manual of freestyle shamanism and sigilization. Suitable for all those inspired by such figures as Austin Spare and Aleister Crowley, and the imperative to develop one's own unique magical way.

Nadia Choucha's *Surrealism and the Occult*
1991 140pp 1869928-164, £8.99 pbk 16 Plates
Many people associate Surrealism with politics, but it was also permeated by occult ideas, a fact often overlooked by art historians.
'Highly readable...seminal...fascinating...'
Francis King writing in *Nuit Isis* II,i

Jean Overton Fuller's *Sickert and the Ripper Crimes*
1990, 260pp, 1869928-156 £14.95 hbk (and soon in paperback)
The author draws on the new evidence of Florence Pash, and with her artist's eye discovers clues in Sickert's pictures, pointing conclusively to the true identity of the Ripper...
'new and important evidence..' Colin Wilson in *Hampstead & Highgate Express*

Timothy d'Arch Smith's *The Books of the Beast*
1992 128pp, 1869928-172 £6.99 pbk
The indispensable and authoritative guide to Aleister Crowley's magical first editions. Plus essays on Montague Summers; R A Caton and his Fortune Press; Ralph Chubb; Florence Farr; The British Library Private Case; and the Author himself.

Jean Overton-Fuller's *The Magical Dilemma of Victor Neuburg*
1990 270pp 1869928-121, 11 plates, £9.99,
A biography of Victor Neuburg, poet, magician and lover of Aleister Crowley.
'a fascinating yet immensely sad story'   Martin Booth in *Sunday Telegraph*

Snoo Wilson's *More Light*
1990 96pp, 1869928-083, £4.95 pbk
A play about the heretic Giordano Bruno.

AMOOKOS's *Tantra Magick*
1990 128pp, 1869928-105 £6.99 pbk, 1869928-105
The first three sets of instructions for the East-West Tantrik group AMOOKOS and an introduction to magical Tantra.

Continued--

Michael Magee's *Tantrik Astrology*
1989 128pp 1869928-067 £6.99 pbk
The whole purpose of astrology; that is, to start the process of deconditioning from the individual's fixed mind-set as laid down at birth.

Katon Shual's *Sexual Magick*
1991 128pp 1869928-075 £6.99 3rd Edition
A radical new approach to the subject and one that has inspired a new generation of sexual magicians, whether heterosexual, lesbian or gay.

Aleister Crowley's *Art In America*
1869928-040 £2.50 pbk 16pp
Crowley's essay written for the *English Review* in 1913, gives one very unusual person's view of developing American art.

Nuit-Isis:
The Leading Journal of the Left Hand Path * Tantra * Crowley * Illuminati * Chaos
'Consistently the most intelligent and readable Thelemic publication from abroad, this Journal....never disappoints....' *Abrasax*
Single copy £2.50
Subscriptions: (2 issues)
Europe £5, USA/Canada £6, Institutions & Rest of World £10

Send for a full catalogue of new books published and distributed by Mandrake Telephone Oxford (0865) 243671 or write to PO Box 250, Oxford, OX1 1AP (UK) or fax (0865) 59298 (Orders only)
Order Form:

Please add £1 to cover postage (UK); overseas please add 20% (to a maximum of £8.50 or request proforma)
☐ Enclose a cheque (UK/US Banks only)/Money Order/Currency equivalent at your own risk/Eurocheque made out to Mandrake.
☐ Please debit Access/Visa/Mastercard (Please circle correct card)*

Card No
Expiry Date
Name
Address

Signature